Advance Praise for *Culturally Proficient Education: An Asset-Based Response to Conditions of Poverty*

By **Randall B. Lindsey, Michelle S. Karns, and Keith Myatt**

"Before we can look at our students in a way that emphasizes what strengths and skills they bring to the classroom, we need to look at ourselves, our biases, and preconceptions. This book is an interactive model that uses the tools of cultural proficiency as a lens to look not only at our students, but also ourselves. This self-reflection enables us to be more effective for all our students."

—Rick Mooradian, Teacher
Tahoe Elementary School, Sacramento, CA

"For years, poverty has been described as one of the contributing factors for a lack of academic progress and achievement for a diverse group of low performers, but too few authors take the time to go beyond identifying the problem. Culturally Proficient Education: An Asset-Based Response to Conditions of Poverty *takes the next step and is a necessary tool for any educator or school administrator worried about those under-resourced children who struggle to meet achievement goals. The vignettes are thought provoking and challenged me to be introspective about my own work. I believe that faculties will enjoy the opportunity for rich discourse that the reflective questions provide and an opportunity to look at cultural proficiency, poverty, and the achievement gap using an assets-based lens. From this perspective, children and their families are not blamed, viewed as a problem, or seen as broken and needing to be fixed. This perspective is the organizing premise of the book which then guides educators to collaboration, sharing resources, and strength-based problem solving."*

—Aida Molina, Executive Director
Bakersfield City School District, Bakersfield, CA

"This is a timely topic and one that relates to the work schools must do. The moral imperative of providing every child with a quality education has school leaders examining instructional practices to ensure culturally proficient teaching. The manuscript provides the reader with the context for this need as well as helpful continuums and reflective questions. It does provide thoughtful and insightful questions to enable individuals to examine personal biases, beliefs, and values."

—Rosemarie Young, Principal
Jefferson County Public School, Louisville, KY

"Although I have read other books that are intended to reach a similar audience, I think that this book is not duplicating anything that is currently available. In my opinion, the book is most thought provoking as the reader is forced to examine his or her own beliefs and biases. The explanation of "culturally proficient instructors" and the asset-based perspective from which they approach students, the essential elements of cultural competence which they apply is certainly no less than all students deserve!"

—Amy Allen, Educational Consultant
Baton Rouge, LA

Culturally Proficient *Education*

An Asset-Based Response to Conditions of Poverty

Randall B. Lindsey
Michelle S. Karns
Keith Myatt

Foreword by Dennis Parker

A Joint Publication

CORWIN
A SAGE Company

AMERICAN ASSOCIATION
OF SCHOOL ADMINISTRATORS

For information:

Corwin
A SAGE Company
2455 Teller Road
Thousand Oaks, California 91320
(800) 233–9936
Fax: (800) 417–2466
www.corwin.com

SAGE India Pvt. Ltd.
B 1/I 1 Mohan Cooperative
 Industrial Area
Mathura Road, New Delhi 110 044
India

SAGE Ltd.
1 Oliver's Yard
55 City Road
London EC1Y 1SP
United Kingdom

SAGE Asia-Pacific Pte. Ltd.
33 Pekin Street #02–01
Far East Square
Singapore 048763

Printed in the United States of America

Library of Congress Cataloging-in-Publication Data

Lindsey, Randall B.
Culturally proficient education : an asset-based response to conditions of poverty / edited by Randall B. Lindsey, Michelle S. Karns, Keith Myatt.
    p. cm.
Includes bibliographical references and index.
ISBN 978-1-4129-7086-0 (pbk.)
    1. Children with social disabilities—Education. 2. Poor—Education. 3. Educational equalization. I. Karns, Michelle. II. Myatt, Keith. III. Title.

LC4065.L56 2010
371.826'9420973—dc22   2009051375

This book is printed on acid-free paper.

10   11   12   13   14   10 9 8 7 6 5 4 3 2 1

Acquisitions Editor:	Dan Alpert
Associate Editor:	Megan Bedell
Production Editor:	Eric J. Garner
Copy Editor:	Terri Lee Paulsen
Typesetter:	C&M Digitals (P) Ltd.
Proofreader:	Susan Schon
Indexer:	Judy Hunt
Cover Designer:	Scott Van Atta

Contents

Foreword

Dennis Parker

The greatest educational challenge of our time is upon us. It is to operate schools in a way that makes poverty essentially irrelevant. Can we close the achievement gap between the haves and have-nots? Apparently so. Can we close it on a large scale across the country? That will depend on the will of those in charge of our schools. The guidelines in this book are designed to provoke that will so that certain groups of students are no longer disenfranchised from the promise of success in the Information Age and the global economy.

When we look at the growing number of turn-around schools reported by the likes of Doug Reeves, Mike Schmoker, and Katie Haycock, the theory that poverty causes low achievement in schools must be abandoned. It only *seems* to cause low achievement because of how schools have been run traditionally. Obviously, some educators have found ways to do business that makes it possible for students heretofore doomed to educational failure to succeed well enough to be competitive with their more advantaged peers. Are these educators more charismatic or more intelligent than the rest of us? Not really, but they do act on assumptions, beliefs, and knowledge that open the door to solving the problems and finding the innovations necessary to be successful with low-income kids.

Is there a single formula for such success? Surely not. Can any group of educators get together in their school and begin to figure it out too? Surely they can if they can overcome the barriers—both conscious and unconscious—to the notion that it is actually possible. Fortunately, this book helps us acquire that notion in a variety of ways. Unlike some treatments of this subject that provide us only with the window of insight into the limitations of our beliefs and policies, this book provides us with a doorway to action.

The authors are committed to an asset-based rather than a deficit-based approach. They remind us not to continue to blame the victims and compensate for their shortcomings. Rather, we should find out about their strengths and come to grips with our own blindness related to beliefs, policies, and actions that unwittingly contribute to our failure with them.

What is most striking about this approach, however, is the way it is modeled throughout the book. There are vignettes and case studies that illustrate that putting the onus for students' success back on ourselves can be done without guilt-tripping those of us in charge of running schools. Yes, we are in charge of changing the status quo, but we don't have to feel guilty that we haven't seen the light before now. If you believe as I do that human enterprises such a schooling run primarily and fundamentally on feelings, the lack of blame and guilt in this approach is not only refreshing but absolutely necessary for it to be effective in provoking the insights required to dramatically improve schools for low-income kids.

With the help of a variety of tools such as the "Guiding Principles" and the "Essential Elements of Cultural Proficiency," the authors walk us through an "inside-out" approach, helping us reveal to ourselves the overt and subliminal norms and policies that get in our way. With these tools and examples, anyone can begin the deep conversations necessary to open the way to more effective practices for all children.

In their own way, they help us to achieve a *"conscientização"* through a "dialogic process" as advocated by the late Paulo Freire in his landmark work *Pedagogy of the Oppressed*. Freire believed that the lot of the poor and oppressed was not predestined nor immutable to change. Since the conditions in society are made by man, they can be changed by man. This message by Freire, which is echoed in this work as well, is a powerful statement of both hope and responsibility. It may be uncomfortable to unveil our beliefs, to examine our policies, and to search for new ways to act. But the stakes are too high for "other people's children" for us to fail to act now. I might add that the stakes are also too high for us to continue to fail to fulfill our own sacred calling as educators.

This volume offers a safe, effective road map for doing just that. No matter how uncomfortable or difficult, the implicit message of hope and optimism will lead us to improve the human condition by improving how we school our most vulnerable children. May this book help you in your own quest for adding yet another school to the roles of outlier institutions that have dared to confront poverty and win. Do it for your students. Indeed, do it for yourself!

Acknowledgments

We are deeply appreciative of the many people who have influenced and shaped our lives. Constructing this book was a challenge in that we, the authors, probed our own histories to revisit the many people and events that have served to make our experiences a fundamental part of this book. We are grateful for the support and patience of family, friends, and colleagues who encouraged us at every stage in the development of this book. In constructing this book, we were keenly aware that we are the sum total of our experiences and it has been educators as mentors and as colleagues who started us on our continuous journey to cultural proficiency.

A special thank you goes to Dan Alpert, our acquisitions editor, for being with us in this journey. Dan is more than our editor; he has become a mentor and critical friend as we developed the ideas for our work into this story. Megan Bedell, our associate editor, deserves a thank you for her support and assistance through the many stages in the development of our manuscript into this book.

The preceding work of Terry Cross, Kikanza Nuri-Robins, Raymond Terrell, Delores B. Lindsey, Laraine Roberts, Franklin CampbellJones, Richard Martinez, Stephanie Graham, R. Chris Westphal Jr., Cynthia Jew, Linda M. Jungwirth, Jarvis V. N. C. Pahl, and Brenda CampbellJones is foundational to our thinking that helped construct our manuscript. This book was informed and shaped by their foregoing work on cultural competence and cultural proficiency.

Delores B. Lindsey is deeply appreciated for her significant role in the conceptual and final stages of this book. Delores provided many hours of high-quality feedback on each stage of the final manuscript. Her knowledge of cultural proficiency, editorial skills, and passion for all students having access to high-quality education ensured the significance of this manuscript.

Publisher's Acknowledgments

The contributions of the following reviewers are greatly acknowledged:

Beverly Alfeld
Academic Performance Specialist and Advocate
Crystal Lake, Illinois

Amy Allen
Educational Consultant
Baton Rouge, Louisiana

Scott Currier
Mathematics Teacher
Belmont High School
Belmont, New Hampshire

Barbara Dowling
Elementary School Development and Special Education
Sioux Falls, South Dakota

Peggy Hickman
Assistant Professor
Arcadia University
Glenside, Pennsylvania

Laurie Peterman
Teacher
Andover High School
Lino Lakes, Minnesota

Rosemarie Young
Principal
Jefferson County Public School
Louisville, Kentucky

About the Authors

Randall B. Lindsey, PhD, is professor emeritus, California State University, Los Angeles, and has a practice centered on educational consulting and issues related to diversity. Randy has served as a teacher, an administrator, and executive director of a nonprofit corporation. All of Randy's experiences have been in working with diverse populations, and his area of study is the behavior of white people in multicultural settings. It is his belief and experience that too often white people are observers of multicultural issues rather than personally involved with them. To that end, he designs and implements interventions that address the roles of all sectors of the society.

Randy and his wife and frequent co-author, Delores, are enjoying this phase of life as grandparents, as educators, and in support of just causes.

Michelle S. Karns, MPA, is an educational consultant with over 30 years' experience in school support and reform, including speaking before the United Nations at the World Conference on Children in 1995. Working with students, administrators, and teachers in districts through the United States and Canada, Michelle helps create the conditions for all students to learn and makes academic success complemented by social and emotional health a reality. She is especially successful working in under-resourced, minority districts that are experiencing internal and external challenges.

Michelle combines current academic research and resiliency research in support of hundreds of Title I schools achieving equity and excellence. She is an author of several books and multiple educational reform articles and works to help students and teachers build positive relationships and meet their academic and personal success goals. She is an avid advocate of parents as partners in school reform and is diligent in making that process possible for her districts.

Keith Myatt, MA, teaches educational leadership at California State University, Dominguez Hills in Los Angeles. He is co-president of the California Staff Development Council and works as a consultant in schools with the Center for Data, Collaboration, and Results. Keith has been working in educational leadership since 1992. He served as program director for the California School Leadership Academy (CSLA) for eight years at the Los Angeles County Office of Education. Keith worked with Richard Martinez and Randy Lindsey to coordinate the first Cultural Proficiency Institutes. He has built upon that work as a presenter at the Museum of Tolerance in Los Angeles. Keith will complete his doctoral studies at California Lutheran University in May 2010. His dissertation is the study of a school in a low-income neighborhood with a high concentration of English learners with a high proportion of students reaching grade-level standards in contrast to other schools with similar demographics. He is identifying culturally proficient practices within the school.

I dedicate this book to my best friend, Delores B. Lindsey.

—Randy

I dedicate this book to Roberta Ellis of Tulsa Public Schools. She taught me the Title I and categorical "ropes," and she allowed me to help school administrators create conditions for impoverished, challenged children and their families to begin to learn and grow. And when it was necessary, we flew under the radar to do what was right for kids.

—Michelle

I dedicate this book to the students in the Educational Leadership programs at Dominguez Hills. Their passion and commitment to leading Los Angeles County's most underserved schools is an inspiration and our best hope for the future of our communities.

—Keith

Introduction

At long last, the issue of educating students from low-income or impoverished communities has gained currency! If you are an educator in quest of new and fresh ways to be successful with students from such communities, this may be the book for you. Then again, maybe not! Read on to find out "why" or "why not."

We, the authors of this book, believe that effective approaches with students from low-income or impoverished communities begin with looking inward at ourselves as educators, as well as examining the schools and school systems for which we work. However, when we surveyed current approaches being sold and used in the market, we were struck by how many represent a "deficit approach" that deems our role as educators is to correct the deficiencies in students and, by implication, their parents/guardians.

Cultural proficiency is an "asset-based approach" that begins with the premise that students from low-income and impoverished communities are educable, and it is our role as educators to find out how best to get the job done. A related premise is that educators know the technical aspects of our roles, whether that is as a teacher, a counselor, an administrator, or a policymaker. Cultural proficiency acknowledges these two premises as being central to our effectiveness and adds the dimension of our needing to understand and value the culture of the student for us to develop an educator relationship with the student and the student's community. Though, as you will see in Chapter 3, that we refute poverty as a distinct culture, we do regard low-income and impoverished communities as being comprised of people who have assets that when recognized and valued by their schools, heightens our effectiveness as educators.

Key Terms: Educator and What Happens on Campus

Please note two intentional uses in this book—use of the term "educator" and a focus on "what happens on school campus." We use the term "educator" throughout the book to demonstrate the interdependence of teachers, counselors, administrators, staff members, and trustees and school board members. It is our experience that many efforts to close achievement gaps focus narrowly on changing teacher behavior or in developing principals as instructional leaders. While either approach may have merit, in isolation they too often lead to fragmentation and alienation. In Part I, "educator" is used as an inclusive term to communicate the interdependence of roles. In Part II, we present and discuss our roles as teachers, school leaders (formal and non-formal leaders), and policymakers (formal and non-formal leaders along with elected or appointed trustees and school board members). Part III is devoted to bringing these roles together in a manner that leads to an examination of school and school systems' policies and practices along with educators' values and behaviors.

"What happens on campus" is a central focus of this book. We use Cross's (Cross, Bazron, Dennis, & Isaacs, 1989) term "inside-out approach" to guide our examination of what happens on campus. We make the case that there are socioeconomic conditions that surround our schools that are beyond our direct control, but we do have direct control over what occurs on our campuses. We cite research and academic references, present vignettes, and provide reflective and dialogic questions as opportunities to examine educators' values and behaviors when in service to students and parents or guardians from low-income and impoverished communities. Similarly, you are invited to use these same resources to examine and change policies and practices as needed to be supportive of the education of children and youth within your school community.

We are very pleased to present this book to you and look forward to conversation with you about how the book informs your work and to your suggestions about how we can all get better at doing this very important work. Each of us—Randy, Michelle, and Keith—come to this work from different paths. Two of us are career preK–12 educators and university faculty members and the other is a social worker who has been working with preK–12 schools for several years. Three elements unite us in constructing this book for your use:

- Our belief that students from low-income and impoverished communities have the capacity to learn at high levels.

- Our belief that schools have the capacity to learn how to educate all students.
- Our belief that the styles of democracy in Canada and the United States are most effective when ensuring the rights and opportunities of historically marginalized groups of people.

How to Use This Book

We recommend that you read the chapters that comprise Part I first. Chapters 1 and 2 provide information that you may find edifying and that will inform your conversations and dialogues with colleagues. Should you be familiar with the tools of cultural proficiency, you may want to scan Chapter 3. Then, please read the chapters in Part II. You may want to focus on the chapter that speaks to your current role: Chapter 4 for teachers, Chapter 5 for school leaders, and Chapter 6 for policymakers. If you do focus on your primary chapter, we encourage you to read the other chapters to be familiar with what is being asked of other educators as they internalize inside-out approaches to their roles in your school or school system. Part III is designed for you, individually or collectively with colleagues, to organize your learning into your personal or professional or organizational change initiative.

The Resources section provides you with reference material. Resource A holds the conceptual framework of cultural proficiency and serves to support the presentation of the tools of cultural proficiency as presented in Chapter 3. Resource B presents the script for the State Teachers' Association retreat that a teacher from Pine Hills High School experiences. Resource C is the full text of Taniko's poem, passages of which appear in Chapter 4. Resource D is a matrix of the books about cultural proficiency.

Most important, thank you for your abiding interest in the education of children and youth from low-income and impoverished communities.

PART I

Why Poverty and Cultural Proficiency?

The Intent of This Book

We, the authors, designed this book to address the two major roles we assume as educators—as individual educators and as members of school systems.

- This book is about how we reach deeply within ourselves and care enough to learn how to teach children from low-income and impoverished backgrounds.
- This book is about how we engage with our colleagues to reach within our schools and school systems to create conditions in which children and youth from low-income and impoverished backgrounds achieve at high levels.

Schools in the United States and Canada have the opportunity in the next generation to expand the fruits of democracy in unprecedented ways. In doing so, we will replace a deficit perspective with an asset-based perspective when viewing and working with our students and families from low-income and impoverished communities.

This book is designed for you to use the tools of cultural proficiency to understand the relationship of the culture of schools and schooling to serving communities of low-income and impoverished students and families. Educators who take the time to understand their school's organizational culture in relationship to low-income and impoverished communities are better prepared to recognize and utilize the assets within those communities as building blocks on which to construct successful educational experiences for their children and youth.

We decided to write this book to counter the prevalence of approaches being foisted on schools that build on a deficit perspective. That perspective holds there to be something wrong with people from low-income and impoverished communities that needs to be changed for these students to be successful. We make clear in Chapter 2 that the concept of *culture of poverty* is mythical; however, the culture of schools and schooling is reality. So, this book focuses on the culture of education, schools, and schooling in such a way that prepares us to better serve low-income and impoverished communities.

We recognize that to hold the *culture of poverty* as mythical will be disturbing to many people because it is so much easier to assume poor students who fail in our school do so because of their socioeconomic conditions. Cultural proficiency holds that educators, schools, and school systems have the capacity to be academically successful if we consider change as both a personal and an organizational "inside-out" process. To accomplish personal change in how we work with students and families from low-income and impoverished communities, our inside-out process involves an examination of our values and behaviors and the manner in which these are communicated to our students and their communities. Likewise, school and school system inside-out approaches to change involve examination of policies and practices that directly or indirectly impact our students and their communities.

This book's inside-out approach to change is inspired by Robert Dilts's Nested Levels (1994) of organizational change. The premise of Dilts's model is that change that occurs at one level affects changes at each subsequent, lower level described in the table. Change that occurs at the lowest level of the table may have little impact at each other level in the table.

Table I.1 is important because for too long the tacit assumption in schools that serve students and families from low-income and impoverished communities is that there is something that teachers need to be doing differently that, when provided, should address or remediate the problem of poor academic achievement. We now have several decades of data to demonstrate that approach to be wrong (Perie, Moran, & Lutkus, 2005). During our preparation of this manuscript, Educational Testing Service (Barton & Coley, 2009) issued its

Table I.1 Cultural Proficiency's Inside-Out Approach to Personal and Organizational Change Aligned With Dilts's Nested Levels

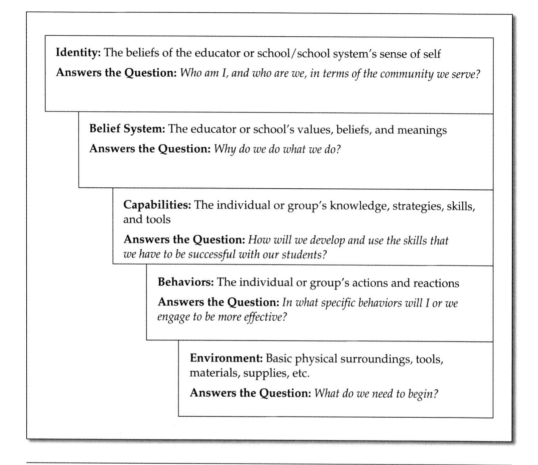

> **Identity:** The beliefs of the educator or school/school system's sense of self
> **Answers the Question:** *Who am I, and who are we, in terms of the community we serve?*
>
> **Belief System:** The educator or school's values, beliefs, and meanings
> **Answers the Question:** *Why do we do what we do?*
>
> **Capabilities:** The individual or group's knowledge, strategies, skills, and tools
> **Answers the Question:** *How will we develop and use the skills that we have to be successful with our students?*
>
> **Behaviors:** The individual or group's actions and reactions
> **Answers the Question:** *In what specific behaviors will I or we engage to be more effective?*
>
> **Environment:** Basic physical surroundings, tools, materials, supplies, etc.
> **Answers the Question:** *What do we need to begin?*

Source: Garmston and Wellman (1999).

most recent and sobering report on the achievement gap and made this important observation:

> The achievement gap has roots deep in out-of-school experiences and deep in the structures of schools. Inequality is like an unwanted guest who comes early in these children's lives and stays late. Policies and practices that are likely to narrow gaps in achievement need to be broad and comprehensive if they are to check inequality at the outset of a child's academic career and create the conditions in which every child can flower and attain in school and in life.
>
> Gains in student achievement can be accomplished at any point along the developmental continuum that efforts are made. And, of course, *formal schooling is where the concentrated effort*

typically is applied to instill knowledge and understanding through an institution solely created for that purpose (emphasis added) (p. 34).

The ETS report observes many factors within society and the educational enterprise that contribute to and can mitigate the negative effects of poverty. With this book we have focused our attention on those factors that we in education have control over, namely the relationship of teaching to learning, leadership support for instruction, and policy development that ensures and supports teaching and learning.

Return to Maple View

This is the fifth *Cultural Proficiency* book in which we have used the Maple View School District as the context for our descriptions and applications of the tools of Cultural Proficiency. Maple View is a fictionalized community created to be the composite of experiences that we and our colleagues have in working with educator and community colleagues devoted to the education of children and youth from all sectors of our society. In this book, we focus on students and their families to tell the stories of intergenerational poverty.

Chapter 1 frames the paradigmatic differences between deficit- and asset-based perspectives on working with students and families from low-income and impoverished communities. The important role of educators working in such communities is described and rationale is provided for merging asset-based perspectives and Culturally Proficient approaches. Chapter 2 describes intergenerational poverty through the eyes of four families and follows them through three generations until they arrive at Pine Hills High School in the Maple View School District. Chapter 3 describes and applies the tools of cultural proficiency. Care is taken in this chapter to describe the paradigmatic shift represented from aligning the Barriers to Culturally Proficient approaches to the deficit-based perspective of working with low-income and impoverished communities in contrast to using the Guiding Principles of Cultural Proficiency to frame asset-based approaches to working with the same communities. With this asset-based perspective, the reader is guided in knowing how the Essential Elements of Cultural Competence are used as standards applied to educator values and behaviors and to schools' policies and practices.

Part II is comprised of Chapters 4, 5, and 6 and covers the topics of teaching and learning, leadership for instruction, and policy development in support of instruction and learning. Part III is a single chapter that is a call to action and provides opportunity for personal and organizational planning.

1

Asset-Based Approaches to Students From Low-Income or Impoverished Communities

When you plant lettuce, if it does not grow well, you don't blame the lettuce.

—Thich Nhat Hanh, 1999, p. 233

Getting Centered

Imagine that you are overhearing the following conversation by two colleagues about students at your school. Pay attention to what they are saying and your reaction to their comments.

Emilia: This issue of our poverty and our students baffles me; I don't know what to make of it.

Jose: What do you mean?

Emilia: Well, the term, *a culture of poverty,*[1] has never worked for me.

Jose: Please tell me that you are kidding. You are, aren't you? You are aware that the kids who come to our school are the products of intergenerational poverty and though it is not their fault, there is precious little we can do other than do our best every day!

Emilia: No, I am not trying to ignore their day-to-day realities, but I don't want to abdicate my responsibilities.

Jose: In plain English, what are you trying to say?

Emilia: To be blunt, I don't know what I am trying to say other than if I carry into my classroom even the notion that their circumstances render them incapable, then haven't I given into those same circumstances? Aren't I saying that I am not capable? Aren't I saying that we as a school are incapable? I am not willing to concede that fact for if I did, I would dread coming here every day.

Jose: So, you are trying to tell me that just the fact of our having lofty intentions and high expectations will end poverty and that all of our students will graduate, go to prestigious schools, and become upstanding citizens?

Emilia: Please, don't go extreme on me. What I am saying is that if I, and by extension all of us at this school, regard our students as capable and worthy of our very best efforts then they will be much better served than if we accept the notion that there is very little we can do.

How do you react to their conversation? What are you thinking? How do you feel about the perspective of each educator? Which perspective is closest to your way of thinking? Take a few moments and record your thinking and feelings about the conversation.

_____

_____

_____

_____

In an earlier book co-authored by one of the authors of this book (Terrell & Lindsey, 2009), we note that Berliner (2005) makes a compelling and chilling case for the intransigence of poverty and its effect on our schools, educational policy, and society. Importantly, Berliner illustrates "the intersection of poverty and race/ethnicity that undercuts the notion prevalent in some professional development circles that the achievement gap is only a socioeconomic issue" (Terrell & Lindsey, 2009, p. 12). That poverty and related socioeconomic issues impact our students, their families, and the services they receive from schools and other agencies is not in dispute. The focus of this book is to acknowledge all factors that impinge on our students and to leverage our energy and resources with the issues over which we have most control and influence.

As Emilia and Jose discovered, terminology often reveals underlying values and attitudes. Terms such as under resourced, poor, lacking in capital, underprivileged, unfortunate, disadvantaged, impoverished, deprived, needy, and poverty-stricken are often used to identify children and youth whose parents and/or guardians are not participating members of the middle class. These same parents are often perceived as unsupportive of their children's education. Too often, the use of such terms derails educator discussions about the needs of students whose circumstances warrant our support. Antonyms that might be used to describe students and communities who are well served in our schools could include resourced, rich, capitalized, privileged, fortunate, advantaged, enriched, indulged, wealthy, and affluent. Of course, those terms are no less stereotypic and often fallacious.

Our schools continue to search for ways to address the educational needs of students from low-income or impoverished communities. For the most part, schools in the United States and Canada since World War II have continuously expanded to educate an increasingly diverse citizenry. The expansion of who gets taught in this country has not been without its travails. The 1954 *Brown vs. Topeka Board of Education* decision by the U.S. Supreme Court brought issues of race into the national consciousness (Franklin & Moss, 1988). Since 1954, judicial decisions, legislative mandates, and executive orders have continued to expand who must be taught to include issues of gender, language acquisition, special needs, and social class.

The Intent of This Chapter

This chapter is about holding the worldview that students from low-income or impoverished communities come to our classrooms and schools with assets upon which we can build. These questions are addressed in this chapter:

- In what ways is poverty manifest in our communities and in our schools?
- To what extent do deficits or assets shape our perspectives about poverty?
- How can one recognize deficit and asset perspectives in ourselves, our colleagues, and in our schools' policies and practices?

- In what ways do culturally proficient practices reflect asset-based perspectives?
- In what ways do the tools of cultural proficiency provide promise in meeting the educational needs of students?

Pogrow (2009) contends that children born into poverty are as capable and bright as anyone else born into our society, and it is our responsibility as educators to find the moral resolve and appropriate strategies to engage all students. To that end, the essence of the conversation in the Getting Centered section of this chapter needs to be occurring in all of our schools serving children and youth from low-income and impoverished communities. Emilia has adopted a lens that holds all students as having value, and she is intentional in aligning her values with her behaviors. To do so, she realizes that current practice is not effective and she is willing to learn whatever is necessary to be successful. Put simply, she believes that she must put forth her best efforts to teach her students and in so doing she involves her own learning. Conversely, Jose appears to hold the notion that the conditions of poverty are so intractable that little can be done in our schools.

Poverty in Our Communities and Schools

Socioeconomic status must be approached as a distinct demographic group within our schools that intersects with, and yet is distinct from, the cultural groups of race, ethnicity, language acquisition, gender, and ableness. This book considers the educational issues of children and youth from low socioeconomic status, or poverty, alongside students' cultural demographic contexts.

Quick: How Many American Kids Are Living in Poverty?

This sub-heading was the title of the section of the weekly newsletter from the Associated Administrators of Los Angeles last summer (Associated Administrators of Los Angeles, 2008). It was a stark, jolting headline presented in bold-face type, alerting its readers of the 2007 Census Bureau finding that 12.5 percent of Americans live in poverty (Hederman, 2008). The U.S. Census Bureau defines poverty in terms of income for families. For example, in 2008, a family of four was determined to be poor if its annual income fell below $21,200. The U.S. Department of Health & Human Services (HHS) provides guidelines for assessing poverty as indicated in Table 1.1.

Of course, data that shows financial parameters does not describe how families currently live or the circumstances that caused their

Table 1.1 2009 U.S. Department of Health & Human Services' Annual Salary Poverty Guidelines

Persons in Family or Household	48 Contiguous States and DC	Alaska	Hawaii
1	$10,830	$13,530	$12,460
2	14,750	18,210	16,760
3	18,310	22,890	21,060
4	22,050	27,570	25,360
5	25,790	32,250	29,660
6	29,530	36,930	33,960
7	33,270	41,610	38,260
8	37,010	46,290	42,560
For each additional person, add	3,740	4,860	4,300

Source: Federal Register (2009, January 23). 74(14), pp. 4199–4201.

poverty. Defining one's poverty circumstance does not tell us what to do to mitigate the condition, nor does it help us reduce the impact on the life of a child. Poverty typically has negative consequences for children, though there are exceptions. For example, families that expect to live in poverty for a period of time seldom internalize the adverse attributes assigned to long-term poverty. The expectation of poverty coupled with a belief that there will be relief in the future seems to buffer or protect families from the detriments of poverty. In fact, beliefs in the future and a sense of purpose about the current reality can serve to mitigate the most difficult circumstances, which seem to be the converse of "a culture of poverty." (Werner & Smith, 1982, 1992, 2001).

Longitudinal resiliency research indicates that individuals possess personal strengths upon which they can rely (Benard, 1991; Garmezy, 1991; Rutter, 1978, 1987; Werner & Smith, 1982, 1992). These strengths can become commodities that students can use in the emotional "stock exchange" negotiated daily. However, most or many of us need to be helped to understand how to use our inner strengths as outer assets. The resiliency research documents what religion and heroes have demonstrated for generations: People survive adversity. No one needs to be a victim to his or her circumstances. Prominent researchers such as Werner and Smith (1982, 1992, 2001), Rutter (1978, 1987), Garmezy (1991), and Masten (2001) demonstrate that the existence of patterns and trends that are uniquely evident in individuals who survive conditions normally thought to engender psychopathology, learning disabilities, or behavioral dysfunction. Furthermore, individuals can be taught how to shift their perspective from what they lost or what has been broken to what is working and what survives and thrives.

As educators, knowing that students arrive at school with assets on which we can build should provide us with a perspective of "what is right" and not "what is wrong."

Reflection

Think of a time when you overcame adversity. What were your strengths on which you relied? Please use the space below to describe the occasion and the strengths you used to overcome the situation.

_____

_____

_____

_____

Think of two of your students or two members of your community. What characteristics have you seen in these two students or adults that have helped them overcome adversity?

_____

_____

_____

_____

In what ways do you believe their and your characteristics are similar? Dissimilar?

_____

_____

_____

_____

Poverty and Learning

Complex relationships exist between poverty and learning. These relationships, when understood by educators, can be used to help students navigate a successful school career in spite of the economic circumstances experienced at home, in the neighborhood, or within the school community. To mitigate poverty, school must be a place where all students feel supported with daily contributions to their future-focused goals and personal social capital. The broader social context of poverty can be managed using prosocial approaches and assets to build new mindsets and future realities. Poverty is not a jail sentence, nor does it have to lead to dysfunction that cripples children for life.

Changing the situation for the students in these schools requires an overhaul in how we think about our students, their circumstances, and our responsibility to influence, change, or impact the status quo. Too often, blaming the students for their low performance, the parents for their socioeconomic conditions, and their race or class for their status in life precludes taking action. The research does not align with these emotionally loaded assignments of blame—students, parents, race, or class do not create low-performing schools (Benard, 2004). Poorly performing schools too often feature low educator expectations, poorly qualified teachers, teachers with limited experience, often lackluster administrators and faculty, and the lack of community support and money for education and youth development (Darling-Hammond, 2004; Delpit, 1995).

Educators, teachers in particular, sell children on their potential futures and the likelihood that they will be okay. Teachers and other adults at the school are in the position to be significant in the lives of many children (Noddings, 2003). For example, educators who use academic standards and assessment results to improve instruction and press for more rigorous curriculum have demonstrated an ability to narrow achievement gaps for students of color and students from low-income backgrounds. The shift in thinking from "our students can't do it" has been replaced by a mindset that says with clear goals, high expectations, rigorous coursework, extra instructional support as needed, and teachers with strong academic and pedagogic backgrounds, "our students can do it" (Wilkins, 2006).

Asset or Deficit Perspectives?

It is our experience that too many educators use poverty or socioeconomic differences as an explanation for underachievement rather than attribute it to any other demographic issues, such as race, ethnicity, language acquisition, or gender. Most state-level accountability and the No Child Left Behind Act (NCLB) systems now require student achievement data to be disaggregated by socioeconomic status in addition to race, language, and gender. Considering socioeconomic issues separate from other demographic groupings provides educators with the opportunity to accurately assess needs and develop programs accordingly. Students' and parental or guardian socioeconomic status must be a visible topic in our schools when discussing achievement, instruction, and curriculum.

Poverty, Accountability, and the Use of Disaggregated Data

If there is a virtue in the No Child Left Behind (2002) requirement to disaggregate data, it is that poverty is not subsumed into the other demographic categories and rendered invisible. Poverty does not become the catchall category for those who want to avoid the disparities in educational attainment associated with race, gender, language, or special needs. As a distinctly separate category, poverty is a social and economic reality for many of our students and their families.

Viewing the education of children and youth from either a deficit- or an asset-based perspective is important in how we choose to approach their education. The accountability movement and the emerging use of disaggregated data provides the opportunity to learn about the assumptions we make about people from low-income and impoverished communities, to select and implement curricular and instruction approaches to meet the learning needs of our students, and to use assessments that inform our progress with these students.

Poverty: Individual or Societal Causes?

Probing our own beliefs about the causes for poverty may be the key to unlocking the extent to which we are successful in working with communities that have a high incidence of poverty. Whether we believe that poverty is caused by individual slothfulness or systemic oppression may dictate the manner in which we approach and work with people from poverty and their children. As important, if we are locked into either of these dichotomous either-or perspectives it may be a predictor of the extent to which we can work within our school systems to mitigate the effects of poverty for the children and youth in our schools. In the United States, beliefs and perceptions about why people are mired in poverty are wide and disparate.

Individualist Perspective. The individualist perspective holds that poverty is caused mainly by individual actions, such as lack of persistence. In other words, people are lazy, unmotivated, and fail to work hard. The individualistic perspective of society holds that we are the architects of our own destinies. Such explanations reflect the dominant, individual perspective of social inequality, which indicates that poverty "is the result of individual inadequacies" and "lies outside the mainstream American experience" (Rank, 2004, p. 6). Indeed, survey evidence shows that "Americans tend to rank individual-level reasons (i.e., laziness, lack of effort, and low ability) as the most important factors related to poverty, while structural reasons such as unemployment or discrimination are typically viewed as less important" (Rank, 2004, pp. 49–50). Beliefs about poverty reflect ingrained ideologies regarding economic opportunity for all, the importance of self-reliance, and the rewards of hard work (Rank, 2004; Weigt, 2006).

Structuralist Perspective. The contrasting structural perspective holds that poverty is created and maintained by social and economic inequities. The structural perspective includes inadequate schools, lack of medical care, low-paying or scarce jobs, weak social safety nets, racism, and discrimination as part of the explanation for conditions of poverty—whether urban or rural (Bullock, Williams, & Limbert, 2003; Galster & Killen, 1995; Prins & Schaft, 2009; Rank, 2004). Rank's structural vulnerability approach uses empirical evidence to show that U.S. poverty results from the "inability of the U.S. labor market to provide enough decent-paying jobs for all families to avoid poverty or near-poverty," coupled with the ineffectiveness of American public policy in reducing levels of poverty via the social safety net" (p. 53).

In truth, the causes of poverty are to a large extent outside the control of most preK–12 educators; however, we can control what occurs within our schools when we have our students with us. We can teach students the skills and knowledge to be the architects of their own destinies and to not buy into a fatalistic viewpoint that holds there is little that can be done to combat insidious forces such as racism or complacency with low-paying jobs. At the same time, we can educate our children, youth, and their community members to become educated about the societal forces that impact their communities and to become organizers to marshal the resources necessary to transform communities.

Recognizing Our Perspectives: Deficit- or Asset-Based?

Understanding poverty and the impact on learning is, for many of us, tantamount to the development of a new pedagogical construct for education. Poverty must not be approached as an excuse or an alibi. It is an economic and social reality that creates a mindset or worldview to be considered as we teach and lead our schools. From our experience, students living in poverty see things differently and experience the world in terms that have limits that too often lead educators to view students from a deficit perspective. This deficit perspective targets what isn't working and what doesn't exist for the child rather than building on the strengths of living in the environment and circumstances. Most children survive their poverty realities and develop full and contributing lives. Our challenge as educators is to develop knowledge and skills to maximize the educational opportunities for children reared in low socioeconomic conditions.

Asset Perspectives Can Be Developed

An asset is identified as a "stock of financial, human, natural, or social resources that can be developed, improved, and transferred across generations" (Ford, 2004 cited in Moser, 2006, p. 5). The five assets most widely known and grounded in empirical research are human, physical, social, financial, and natural capital assets (Moser). Moser cites Ferguson et al. (2006) additionally identifying political assets which are increasingly associated with human rights.

The task of educators, individually and collectively, is to identify and build on students' assets within the realms of our classrooms and schools. It is our belief and observation that we educators are too often constrained by thinking and practice that views our students by "who they are not" or "what they don't have" rather than "what it is they bring to school on which we can build." Then, over time, these deficit ways of thinking inform policy and determine curricular choices, school reform approaches, and the recruitment and placement of our teachers and administrators that reinforces the notion of a second-class citizenry for people from poverty.

Fortunately, asset-based approaches to educational practice and policymaking are not new, just not widely shared. Simply stated, asset-based approaches to education begin with the recognition and appreciation of the student in their own environment. Wiggington (1972) sought to interest rural Appalachian students in English by engaging them in things that interested them. It turned out to be their communities. Two generations later, Gutstein (2006, 2007) used the same approach with marginalized students in Chicago, Illinois. Both educators were successful with their students in ways that were considered non-traditional and counter to the norms of their schools. In other words, Wiggington and Gutstein recognized that current practices were not effective and chose to put students central to their educational planning.

Prior to Wiggington and Gutstein, John Dewey (1916/1944), the pioneer of progressive education, held education to be the means by which society is transmitted from generation to generation. He unabashedly held the future of democracy was within our approaches to educating the citizenry. If the notion of education being central to the transmission of society was true as Dewey proclaimed in the 1916 edition of his book, one can only imagine the importance of education in these first years of the 21st century.

Since Dewey's time, our society has changed in fundamental ways that include:

- Compulsory education through high school graduation has become the requirement in most states of the United States and provinces of Canada.
- Educational equity efforts have sought to end apartheid-like educational systems throughout the United States that denied or severely limit equitable opportunities to African American, First Nations, English Learner, differently abled, and female children and youth.
- An ever widening portion of our under age 18 youth are attending school which has increased the proportion of students from poverty backgrounds being in school.
- State and federal accountability measures, such as No Child Left Behind, the 2002 authorization of the Elementary and Secondary Education Act, have made public disparities in educational attainment in terms of poverty, race, gender, language learners, and ableness.

Deficit Perspective as "Normal"

You might ask that if we are to focus on "assets," then why even deal with issues of "deficit perspective and thinking?" The answer is basic, when referring to people from low socioeconomic or impoverished conditions; deficit thinking permeates our schools and society. A high school educator colleague of ours describes the tendency toward deficit thinking best for us. After studying the tools of cultural proficiency, he noted that he was beginning to hear the comments of colleagues in new ways. He was surprised and dismayed at the negative tone of the comments made about students in his school. When pressed about how he was going to confront his colleagues, he made a very important observation. He commented that the negative climate at the school was so pervasive that he had accepted it as normal. What was important was this time he didn't let those negative comments pass through his memory. His "breakthrough" was now that he could *hear* the negativity; he had the opportunity and the responsibility to reframe conversations from pessimistic to optimistic.

In our preK–12 schools, too often we hear these terms used to describe our students:

- At-risk students
- Socioeconomically disadvantaged students
- Title I students

- Children of poverty
- "Minority" students (when they are the majority in the school, neighborhood, community)
- "Trailer Park" kids
- "Projects" kids
- Kids from over at "the" apartments

When you hear, or use, phrases such as these, what are the mental images that emerge for you about the students being described? Please use the space below to describe those mental images.

_____

_____

_____

_____

Make no mistake; the phrases above are well known by our colleagues in colleges and universities as well as by our educational policymakers. If anything, our higher education and policymaker colleagues even added a new phrase to describe the phrases above. They have added the phrase *deficit approaches or models* as a means to categorize the negative terms for our students.

What Does the Literature Tell Us About Asset-Based Perspectives?

Asset-based thinking frees educators to shake off the belief of deficit-based thinking that stunts our own growth as educators and as people. In our review of the literature about asset-based thinking, we discovered that they grouped naturally into two categories: literature that focuses on how we can change the values and behaviors of our students and literature that focuses on our values and behaviors as educators. The two sets of literature are not necessarily dichotomous as both can be useful. However, too often we encounter an overreliance on changing the values and behavior of our students and their parents or guardians as if they were a problem. Such thinking dangles dangerously close to the precipice of "deficit-based thinking" when it does not focus, at the same time, on the need for a values and behavior change on the part of educators.

The popular literature on working with students from low-income and impoverished communities focuses on how we as educators change/improve the values and behaviors of our students to make them, our students, to be "better" than they are right now (Payne, 2009;

Valencia, 2009). Through the use of empirical study methods, developmental assets have been identified and are grouped into external and internal factors (Scales, Benson, Roehlkepartain, Sesma Jr., & van Dulmen, 2006; Sesma & Roehlkepartain, 2003; Paxis Institute, 2001). The external factors of support, empowerment, boundaries and expectations, and constructive use of time are paired with the internal factors of commitment to learning, positive values, social competencies, and positive identities. The primary focus of these approaches is on how to assist, support, or improve life for our students, which are worthwhile and important goals, to be sure. However, we find it limiting that the suggestion is that students' underlying values are inherently deficient and in need of remediation.

In contrast to the popular literature (Payne, 2005, 2009; Valencia, 2009), scholars have been consistent in illustrating that the change begins with we the educators in how we perceive, value, and work with our students (Freire, 1998; Ladson-Billings, 1994; Spring, 2006). Noddings may have summarized it best with her now well-known ethic of care when she wrote in 1992, "The first job of the schools is to care for our children" (Shapiro & Stefkovich, 2005, p. 17). Please take note of the use of the inclusive phrase *our children.* Our approach, using the three-tiered framework described above, is to understand our underlying and often unrecognized assumptions about low-income and impoverished communities and how we can direct ourselves to be influential in the lives of our students in intentional ways.

The No Child Left Behind Act (2002) is the first time in the history of the United States that states and schools are held accountable for all students being academically successful (Chenoweth, 2007; Lindsey, Graham, Westphal Jr., & Jew, 2008). Chenoweth set out to find schools that demonstrated that all children can learn (vii). Her study of 14 schools representing broad demographic diversity found that these schools did not use poverty as a reason for students not succeeding. In fact, she cited principals in Chicago and Detroit who were infused with a "sense of possibility and a belief that the job they have taken is worth doing" (ix). Chenoweth observed that the often referenced 1966 Coleman Report's finding that family background has a strong predictive role in student achievement and, by dubious extrapolation, has led many educators to believe there is little that schools can do to mitigate the negative effects of poverty (p. 7). Her study of schools that were "unexpectedly successful" found that educators were intentional and proactive in finding and using instructional strategies and approaches to working with students that offset the ill effects of poverty and discrimination on academic achievement.

The Promise of Culturally Proficient Approaches

To meet the educational access and achievement needs of students from low socioeconomic backgrounds, the cultural proficiency approach to assets development aligns well with "resiliency research." Resiliency studies are consistent with recent work from cultural proficiency in its reliance on an inside-out approach to learning for both the educator and the child or youth. Werner and Smith (1992) noted that resilience is one's inner capacity for making decisions that lead to appropriate changes in one's behavior. Chapter 3 presents the tools of cultural proficiency and describes the inside-out nature of personal and organizational transformation.

The relationship between children and nurturing adults is significant. In our schools, educator-student relationships shape how students create their worldview, future plans, and expectations of themselves and others. Benard (1991) held that caring adults demonstrate interest in their students through engaging in listening that engenders trust, looking for students' strengths rather than their deficits, and through involving students in activities that 'give back' to their communities. It is important for students from low-income and impoverished communities to have teachers that care about them and about their communities. Recognizing and acknowledging students' and their communities' assets fosters respect and trust that they can be the architects of their own futures.

The culturally proficient approach for asset development in our children and youth focuses clearly on our role as educators. We can mitigate the negative, external forces that impact our students by focusing on what we can do in our classrooms, schools, and school districts to develop and support healthy students. In simple terms, we concentrate on the seven hours students are on our campus and where we have most influence rather than on the 17 hours that students are not on campus and over which we have literally no control and precious little influence. The focus of this approach is on our values and behaviors as individual educators and on the policies and practices of our classrooms, schools, and school districts.

Poverty in Canada and the United States is historical and is based in social, economic, and political forces. Poverty is described as generational, evidence of economic and societal inequities, urban or rural in locale, or evidence of discrimination or indolence (Prins & Schaft, 2009). Educational programs designed to support children and youth from impoverished backgrounds often speak of developing resilience within students in order for them to survive and thrive in our schools and the larger society (Benard, 1991; Noddings, 2003). The important first step is for educators to be aware of how our beliefs about poverty influence our interactions with our students and, then, to be able to view our students as capable of learning.

Table 1.2 provides a preview of the culturally proficient approach to asset-based development by showing it in contrast to the too prevalent deficit-based approach. Chapter 3 describes the four tools of cultural proficiency and illustrates how we move from the left side to the right side of Table 1.2.

Table 1.2 Cultural Proficiency Conceptual Framework Asset-Based Perspectives on Issues of Poverty

Destructiveness, Incapacity, Blindness	Precompetence, Competence, Proficiency
Deficit-Based Perspective • Other directedness • Find reason to blame and shame • Fix what is perceived to be broken and needing to be fixed • Sometimes issues cannot and should not be fixed—color, language, etc. • Views education as "Windows" to look at the problems	Asset-Based Perspective • Personal and community scales • Focus on own skill or will issues • Build on what others know and do • View culture as a building block, not a liability • View education as "Mirrors" to examine assumptions and devise new approaches
• Compliance focused	• Advocacy • Future focused • Commitment to social justice • Commitment to life-long learning
• Isolated working by adults, therefore the students. Non-productive and/or toxic • "I've done as much as I can do"	• Professional Learning Communities • "What's the next thing I can do?"
Systems • Private practice, work in cliques. Toxic • Use the teacher's edition • Misread what they are supposed to be doing; misread the audience, intent, purpose	Systems • Quality relationships—prosocial and proactive such as learning communities invested in one another's successes • Meaningful work—mission • Future focus—what we are to become (vision)
Lack of Resilience • Isolated • Humorless • Other directed; victim • Shortsighted • Dependent • Rigid • Plateau • Stunted	Resilience • Relationships • Humor • Inner direction • Perceptiveness • Independence • Interdependence • Flexibility • Learning • Efficacious • Self-worth • Faith or spirituality • Perseverance • Creativity

Alberto, Tina, and Darren

Alberto, Tina, and Darren are three high school students at Pine Hills High School, with Emilia as one of their teachers. Each student has a different history and story but share a similar experience of living in low-income or impoverished conditions.

Alberto is a 15-year-old sophomore. He is an English learner and reads at the seventh-grade level and has the vocabulary of a middle grades student. Sometimes he gets so frustrated he lashes out at anything that gets in his way. He has been through Student Study Teams, has an Individualized Education Plan, and has been involved in many mentor programs. His data has been analyzed and plans have been drafted at nearly every juncture in his educational career. He has been a kid in crisis, at risk of failure, and likely to be a dropout of school, but he has begun to blossom this school year. His family struggles to stay together. His mother works, but she makes so little they can hardly keep the rent paid and dinner on the table.

Tina, another 15-year-old, has one younger brother and one older sister. She has never lived in an apartment longer than one year. Her friends' parents don't want their children to come to her house and sometimes they don't want her around theirs. Her mother makes scenes at school events and doesn't seem to care that she is embarrassing her kids. Though quiet, Tina is really smart and athletic. Some of her friends' parents make sure that she has what she needs. Tina has decided that she wants to go to a prominent, local state university. She does everything she can to make sure that the adults around her know of her future plans. She constantly asks for advice and tries to prepare for being on her own.

Darren has three siblings. He is the oldest, at age 16, and has to stay home from school if anyone is sick. The truth is that most of the time the kids in his neighborhood *want* to go to school no matter what happens because that is where two out of the three meals that they eat during the day are provided. They take as much food home as they can hide in their backpacks. Sometimes that is really hard because they have a rule at school that you are not supposed to take any food out of the cafeteria. But there is so much food that people just throw away! Darren doesn't see any harm in taking some of it. Food and survival are the primary concerns for this student. For Darren, getting schoolwork done is a secondary responsibility.

Each of these students currently attends Pine Hills High School, a Title I school where free and reduced-price lunch exceeds 80 percent and the AYP (Adequate Yearly Progress, a federal measure of academic achievement) is a constant struggle to attain and maintain. The educators are the most significant resources to mitigate the effects of poverty and engender success in academic pursuits, social interactions, and future-focused planning. Teachers meet poverty head-on every day at Pine Hills High School where Alberto, Tina, and Darren attend school.

Looking for Students' Assets

The principal of Pine Hills High School prevailed upon the School Leadership Team to hire a consultant who has been working with the Maple View School District on issues related to equity in education. The consultant has been interviewing students who had improved two or more performance levels on the state-required standards test. One such student was Alberto. While interviewing Alberto, the consultant noted that he was small of stature, that he spoke clearly and well, and that he seemed thoughtful in choosing his words. His response to her query, "Why do you get such good grades?" surprised her in that he said, "My teacher stood up for me."

Alberto proceeded to describe a situation that occurred in Emilia's class. Several of the other students had been making fun of him when his response to a question she had directed to the class was obviously wrong. Emilia immediately stepped into the middle of the classroom and made it clear that making fun of one another was not allowed in this classroom. Alberto had not experienced a teacher being so forthright in enforcing classroom rules. "What was interesting," said Alberto, "was the other students backed off and didn't hassle me anymore. For me, nothing was ever the same again, because my teacher made sure that I learned everything." He intoned, "She made sure I got it!"

The consultant reflected on notes from her interview with Alberto and other students who reported similar, constructive experiences with Emilia. She decided to interview Emilia to see if she was using extraordinary strategies with her students. Emilia responded, "No, I just treat my students the way I want my children to be treated." After the interview, the consultant summarized her notes into these recommendations:

- Try to codify what it means "to treat students as if they were your own children."
- Help teachers see the value of making themselves accessible so students can ask for help in a less public forum than the classroom.
- Help create the conditions where it is absolutely expected that educators believe in the worth of every student.

In Chapter 2 you will be introduced to the grandparents and parents of Emilia, Alberto, Tina, and Darren. Chapter 2 uses these four people to trace historical and generational poverty right into our classrooms. We will follow the transformation of Emilia in Chapters 4, 5, and 6 as we describe the efforts of teachers, school leaders, and policymakers in responding to the needs of children and youth from low-income and impoverished communities.

Going Deeper

If this book is to be useful to you it should engender questions, comments, observations, or wonderings for you. The following questions can guide your own thinking and be used with a faculty book study.

What in this chapter resonated for you or you found of interest?

_____

_____

_____

_____

What do you view as the main ideas of the chapter?

_____

_____

_____

_____

In what ways does the information in this chapter apply to you and your role as an educator?

_____

_____

_____

_____

After reading this chapter, what would you like to analyze further (it may be about the content of the chapter, or it could be about your and your school's practices)?

_____

_____

_____

_____

In what ways does this view of working with students from low-income or impoverished communities compare with your prior knowledge?

_____

_____

_____

_____

What commitments are you able to make about working with students from low-income or impoverished communities?

_____

_____

_____

_____

Educator Tip. The questions above are derived from Bloom (2007) and can be applied to in-classroom use as well as educator reflection or professional development. Beginning with the first question, the questions are of these types: recall, understand, apply, analyze, evaluate, and create.

Note

1. The term *culture of poverty* emerged from the 1959 work of anthropologist Oscar Lewis, where he introduced the term *subculture of poverty* as a way of describing how people became socialized to adapt to societal inequities.

2

The Middle Class School in Communities of Poverty

Of all the preposterous assumptions of humanity over humanity, nothing exceeds most of the criticisms made on the habits of the poor by the well-housed, well-warmed, and well-fed.

—Herman Melville, Quote in
Toronto *Globe and Mail*, 2009, p. L6

Getting Centered

Note: This first section is intended to be provocative! This chapter illustrates the contrast of our reality as educators with that of our students from low-income and impoverished communities.

Keep an open mind and be aware of your thoughts and reactions as you read this opening section. You are provided an opportunity to record your thoughts and reactions following these passages.

Most of us who are educators and work in communities with high rates of poverty lead lives characterized by *our* day-to-day realities in that we

- Drive or commute from our homes to schools located in communities of poverty
- Have health insurance
- Have guaranteed pensions
- Have predictable monthly incomes
- Work in institutions that reflect middle class values and standards
- Have not experienced poverty for an extended period in our lives

In contrast to our life experiences, consider data provided by the Children's Defense Fund (2008) titled "Each Day in America for Children," which reflects the intensity of poverty every day:

- 2,583 babies are born into poverty.
- 753 white, non-Hispanic babies are born into poverty.
- 794 black babies are born into poverty.
- 956 Latino babies are born into poverty.
- 88 Asian and Pacific Island babies are born into poverty.
- 52 American Indian and Alaska Native children are born into poverty.
- 60 are mixed heritage and/or not identified by ethnicity or race.

Given the persistent nature of people living in conditions of poverty, one of the predictable patterns of being born into poverty is the lessened access to health care and adequate schools, and having parents/guardians who are underemployed. Please note the contrast between our daily realities as educators, represented at the opening of this section, and what must be the daily reality of our students and their parents/guardians who live in low-income or impoverished communities.

Reflection

Though you may or may not be surprised by the Children's Defense Fund data, what thoughts and reactions did you have as you read the descriptions of our lives as educators and the data that describes the communities we serve? What questions are with you? Please use the space below to record your responses.

_____

_____

_____

_____

The Intent of This Chapter

In this chapter we provide descriptions of

- The nature of being from a low-income or impoverished community in Canada and the United States over the last century.
- The expansion of compulsory education from the earliest part of the 20th century into these early years of the 21st century.
- The dawn and expansion of the education accountability movement.
- Cultural proficiency as an asset-based approach to education.

To assist in relating these topics to real life students, we introduce formally the grandparents and parents of Emilia, Alberto, Tina, and Darren. Through their intergenerational stories, we trace the persistence of poverty through the children and youth from four communities. As you read this chapter, pay particular attention to the changing, evolving role of schools and your reaction to the information in the chapter.

Faces in the History of Poverty

Living in low-income and impoverished communities has been a common experience for many people in Canada and the United States throughout our histories. The last century has been witness to internal and external migrations of people that was parallel to economies that moved from primarily agricultural to industrial to technological. Accompanying the changes in the economic structure of our countries has been an often rapidly changing role of preK–12 schools.

Early 20th Century

The early part of the 20th century was characterized by a much broader social class structure than we have today. The rich were rich; the poor were in service to the rich, or worked as farm laborers, or worked in factories and had little chance of moving from low-income or impoverished conditions unless they had extraordinary tenacity, innate talent, intellectual capacity, or a generous sponsor. It was not until the post–World War II period that the middle class, as we know it today, emerged. Life in the early 20th century was close to the land and, even though urbanization was well under way, most population was centered in rural areas and small towns. A rudimentary education served the needs of most people and their employers.

The stories of the four people described later in this chapter are reflective of U.S. census data reported in 1920. Table 2.1 indicates that about two-thirds of children and youth were attending school, at any level. The reality for African American and foreign-born whites indicated fewer than half were attending school. It is important to recognize that failure to attend school, then as now, increased the likelihood that a person would be poorly educated with diminished options in life. Formal education remained the one way to gain literacy skills that might support one having the choice to move away from the conditions of poverty.

Table 2.1   1920 Census: Students Ages 5–20 Attending School by Gender, Race, Native or Foreign Born, and Mixed Race Expressed in Percentage (Using Designations From 1920 Census)

Population	School Attendance in Percentage		
Total Population	Both Genders	Male	Female
All classes	64.3	64.1	64.5
Native white of native parentage	66.9	66.6	67.3
Native white of foreign or mixed parentage	65.8	66.0	65.7
Negro	53.5	52.4	54.5
Foreign-born white	44.2	45.8	42.7

Source: Fourteenth Census, Vol. III, United States, Table 2. 04097225no5ch1.pdf page 3 of 146

An Un-Level Education Playing Field

Our schools, like the society in which they are nested, continued to reflect systemic inequities. They have from the beginning of our country. As a result of French sociologist Alexis de Tocqueville's tour of the United States in the 1830s (de Tocqueville, 2001), his observation that the social mobility in the United States with no parallels in European countries has continued to be perpetuated as part of a national myth. (In using the term *myth*, we intend it as communicating a cultural story.) Social mobility was the experience of many western and northern European immigrants of the 19th century, but people from the First Nations, slaves and the progeny of slaves, and most women found social mobility to be grudgingly slow. While many immigrants moved into the burgeoning middle class in two to three generations, most 19th century citizens were locked into low-wage jobs and provided little if any formal education (Takaki, 1991). Basic rights of citizenship that were guaranteed

to property-owning white men with the signing of the U.S. Constitution
were extended to others only after exhaustive use of the legal processes
afforded by that same Constitution. In effect, all people other than property-owning white men have had to be amended into the social contract
and provided the opportunity to vote, own property, and receive equitable schooling (Franklin & Moss, 1988).

The late 19th century and early 20th century witnessed many
judicial decisions and legislative acts that influenced access to and
quality of education:

- Fresh in the memory of most middle-aged African American
  adults in the early 20th century was the *Plessy vs. Ferguson*
  U.S. Supreme Court (1896) decision that validated the separa-
  tion of black and white pupils and established the "separate
  but equal" doctrine (Franklin & Moss, 1988).
- The Smith-Lever Cooperative Extension Act (1914) established
  the Cooperative Extension system of county agriculture agents.
  The systems were to communicate new technologies from the
  United States Department of Agriculture directly to farmers
  (http://www.ca.uky.edu/agripedia/glossary/smithlev.htm).
- The Smith-Hughes Vocational Act (1917) provided funds to
  support agriculture, industry, and home economics education
  and created the Federal Board for Vocational Education.
- By 1918 compulsory school-attendance laws were in force in
  every state. However, the laws varied in terms of the amount of
  time students were to be in school. In some states, attendance
  laws were not enforced. While the national average for the
  school year was 168.3 days, the average attendance per student
  was 132.5 days. In 1924, 52 percent of what was reported as
  "non-white" were enrolled in school in the United States. Sixty-
  five percent of white students aged 5–19 were enrolled.
- The G.I. Bill (1944) paved the way for the modern middle class and
  the avenue out of low-income and poverty for many, mostly white
  people. (Turner & Bound, 2002; U.S. Department of Veterans
  Affairs, Servicemen's Readjustment Act of 1944). The purpose of
  the G.I. Bill was to ensure transitions for returning soldiers that
  provided them with a place to live and a way to get job training or
  an education. The G.I. Bill continues to be a low-income and
  poverty off-ramp for many veterans and their families.
  Reauthorized in 2009, the G.I. Bill guarantees housing, loans, and
  educational benefits to veterans, their families, and their children.

The wheels of democracy continued to turn in the first half of the
20th century. Judicial decisions and legislative acts served to expand

government-sponsored education in response to a changing economic and social landscape. The changing economic structure of our countries fostered an expanding middle class but did not eliminate low-income and impoverished communities. Though predominately white, the lower socioeconomic groups in Canada and the United States remain disproportionately populated by people of color (Takaki, 1991).

Middle and Latter 20th Century

Post–World War II Canada and the United States were witness to an economic, political, and social expansion of unprecedented proportions. However, the expansion of those benefits was as uneven as had been the "playing field" previously described. The end of the war not only brought to end the terrible carnage of a world war, but it was also witness to the end of the worldwide economic depression that engulfed the decade of the 1930s. The children who grew up in the '30s and '40s were not affected equally by a devastating depression and the ravages of a world war. As these children grew to adulthood, exploding Western economies created a need for a very different workforce to fuel pent-up consumer demand. The shift from needing workers for labor-intense agriculture and industries to needing a more formally educated workforce created an expansion of people not only completing high school, but also attending two-year and four-year colleges. As one might imagine, in the period of the 1950s and 1960s, many were the first in their families to attend, let alone graduate from college.

Table 2.2 shows a dip from the 1920 census in children and youth attending school, which may have been affected by the Depression

Table 2.2   1951 Census: School Attendance of Persons 5–24 Years Old Expressed in Percentage by Age, Color, and Gender (Using Designations From 1951 Census)

Population	School Attendance in Percentage		
Total Population	Total	Male	Female
Total	57.7	58.6	56.9
White	58.3	59.2	57.4
Nonwhite	53.4	53.4	53.3

Source: U.S. Bureau of the Census, Statistical Abstract of the United States 1951, 72nd Edition: Washington, DC, 1951. Table No. 121, page 105 [(1951–02.pdf (105 of 156)]

of the 1930s and World War II. Just over 50 percent of adults were attending school, with over 40 percent who didn't attend school. Failure to attend school, then as now, contributed to a disproportionate percentage of low-income and impoverished youth being prepared for menial work at best.

Equity Movements and Challenges to the Un-Level Playing Field

The latter half of the 20th century was witness to unprecedented challenges to the educational social order:

- Fostered by the 1954 *Brown vs. Topeka Board of Education* U.S. Supreme Court decision (Franklin & Moss, 1988) that invalidated the practice of separate but equal schools, the United States embarked on an often-painful process of desegregating its schools. Though most school districts throughout the United States have dismantled past practices of segregation, inequity continues to persist in terms of students' academic success in our schools.
- The Civil Rights Act of 1964, the Elementary and Secondary Act (ESEA) of 1965, and myriad corresponding pieces of legislation sought to address issues of equity in the United States. One of the pillars of President Lyndon Johnson's "War on Poverty," ESEA was designed to reduce or eliminate funding inequities for schools serving poor communities, a lack of systematic accountability resulted in billions of dollars being spent with uneven results and a lack of impact on chronically underserved schools.
- Current accountability movements, such as those fostered in No Child Left Behind (the current iteration of ESEA), are intended to hold schools accountable for all students being academically successful.

The extent to which the current accountability movements are successful is a matter of much debate. What is not debatable, however, is that for the first time in the history of Canada and the United States educators are acknowledging access and achievement disparities in unprecedented ways. Though progress has been made, to be sure, gaps in access and achievement still doggedly persist.

Table 2.3 shows in 2000 a high percentage of children and youth are attending preK–12 schools, at any level. The data indicate only students attending school and belie an achievement gap that was not well documented until late in the 20th century (see Figure 2.1).

Table 2.3 2000 Census: School Enrollment by Race, Hispanic Origin, and
Age and Sex Expressed in Percentage Total 5–24 Year Olds
(Using Designations From 2000 Census)

	School Enrollment Rate				
Age	**White**	**Hispanic Origin**	**Black**	**All Male**	**All Female**
5–6	96.0	93.3	95.3	95.1	96.1
7–13	98.9	98.9	98.9	98.1	98.3
14–15	98.9	96.8	98.8	98.7	98.6
16–17	95.1	89.1	92.9	92.7	92.9
18–19	66.8	61.1	40.3	58.3	64.2
20–21	48.9	25.6	39.9	41.0	47.3

Source: U.S. Bureau of the Census: 2000, Washington, DC, 2001. Table No. 246, page 155 [sec04.pdf. (7 of 50)]. Retrieved June 1, 2009, from http://www.census.gov/compendia/statab/cats/education.html

Figure 2.1 School Enrollment by Race, Hispanic Origin, and Age and Sex:
2000 Total 3- to 24-Year-Olds (47,673,000)

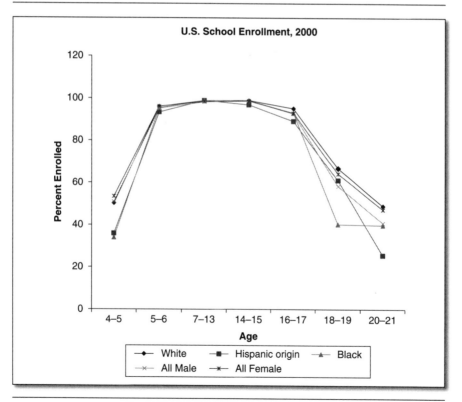

Source: U.S. Bureau of the Census: 2000 Washington, DC, 2001. Table No. 246, p. 155.

Note: In the U.S., the number of 5- to 16-year-olds enrolled in school is fairly even. But in preK and post-11th grade, the percentage enrolled is lower for blacks and Hispanics.

Personal Reflection

What is your personal story? In what ways have you known about or experienced poverty? How does your experience compare or contrast to the information in this chapter?

_____

_____

_____

_____

Professional Reflection

What thoughts are occurring to you as you get to this point in the chapter? What questions do you have about the community you serve? What more would you like to know about your community? What would you like the parents/guardians in your school to know about your school? What would you like the parents/guardians in your school to know about you as an educator?

_____

_____

_____

_____

Accountability: For Whom?

How education is delivered is an emergent question in our society. Many of us who have been educators for a generation or more have been witness to the birth and growth of alternative and charter schools in response to finding better ways to educate all children and youth. Underlying the press for alternate ways to deliver education is the question of assessment and accountability. The question being addressed in this book is to and for whom is accountability addressed?

The beginning stages of accountability began in the 1970s with measures designed to find ways to ensure that students learned the basics of reading and computing. The latter part of the 20th century and this early part of the 21st century has moved the question to making educators and schools accountable. Early in the NCLB era it was vogue to talk of reconstituting schools and even though some schools were reconstituted, it was soon apparent that reconstituting schools was not a feasible, national answer to achievement gap concerns.

A by-product of the assessment movement has been to question the purpose of schooling. As we do so, it is important to heed the words of Gert Biesta (2007) and concentrate on developing democratic citizens rather than developing students as products to be folded into a national economic system. Approaching education as developing young people into citizens capable of charting their own way in the world necessarily begins with viewing them as capable people with assets on which education is built.

Reflection

What do you want for the children and youth in your school that would be different from what you want for your own children, nieces or nephews, cousins, or neighbors?

_____

_____

_____

_____

In the 21st Century

In some ways, poverty of the 21st century mirrors the early part of the 20th century. Persistent poverty is combined with immigration patterns that have brought millions of working poor to our countries in search of a better life (Passel & Cohn, 2008). The current accountability movement did not discover poverty; it has always been there, in unacknowledged ways. The challenge for schools in the 21st century is the extent to which we embrace the mandate to educate all children and youth. To do so requires soul searching on the part of our schools and those of us who are the educators within those schools. To be effective in educating students from communities of poverty requires an examination of our assumptions about our students, a willingness to learn the assets our students and their cultures bring to our classrooms and schools, and the ability to learn knowledge and skills that transfer to our students. When we do these things, our students increase their ability to make their lives what they want them to be.

Four Stories Repeated Throughout Canada and the United States

The story that follows is a fictitious composite inspired by many people we have known and worked with through the years. You will meet Michael, an immigrant from Italy, who could have been from most any part of the world. His story is characteristic of the movement up the socioeconomic ladder in a generation or two. Charles, an African American from the southern United States, who migrated along with thousands of others seeking a better life to the northern and western regions of the United States or in Canada. His story is distinctive in that it epitomizes the alignment of social class and race for most of our national histories.

Following Charles is James Robert, who is from the Appalachian region of eastern Tennessee but could have been from isolated rural regions of Maine, Michigan, Montana, Manitoba, or Ontario. James Roberts' story is of the presence of poverty that persists in the white community. Teresa is an immigrant from Mexico, who today could be from any region of Latin America. Teresa's story entails issues of social class intertwined with ethnic and language issues. In many ways, Teresa could be First Nations and represent any of the many tribal groups extant in Canada and the United States.

In telling these stories, we knowingly focus on four prominent cultural groups to the exclusion of many other ethnic, racial, gender, religious, and ableness cultural groups locked into the invisible caste system that persists in Canada and the United States. It is our intent, and hope, that in focusing on the stories of Michael, Charles, James Robert, and Teresa that we will fulfill the purpose of this book, which is to demonstrate that poverty and social class are not, in and of themselves, barriers to success in our schools.

While we are persuaded by the cogent work of David Berliner (2005) that there are political and social factors outside the influences of day-to-day schooling that impact people of poverty in inhumane ways, we believe that educators can demonstrate that within the daily seven hours students are on our campuses there is much we can do to accomplish equitable access to educational opportunities (Barton & Coley, 2009). Biesta (2007), in presenting different approaches to democratic education, argues that schooling can be most successful when students learn about themselves in the context of society and how to shape and mold that reality. To that end, Michael, Charles, James Robert, and Teresa are the "EveryPerson" (of course, with appropriate apologies to the morality plays of the European Middle Ages) for the faces of poverty in our schools.

Michael

Michael's parents were married in a small Catholic church in Calabria, Italy, in 1917. Their wedding picture shows a young couple, he standing, she seated surrounded by a wedding party of friends and siblings dressed in their finest suits and dresses. They migrated to Tresco, Pennsylvania, because there was work in the coal-mines. In their journey their last name had a vowel and a comma removed from their name. Michael was the fourth of what would have been six siblings had the youngest not died of influenza while an infant.

Michael entered first grade at the age of six with 24 other Italian and Polish children, most had been born in Tresco and their fathers worked the mines. Michael still has his school pictures from each grade and remembers the names of his teachers. Like his older sister Michael was very bright, good with numbers, inquisitive, and polite. On his report cards teachers referred to him as attentive, well-behaved, and good with arithmetic. At the age of 10 in 1934, Michael was almost finished with grammar school and would soon be moving on to something that had been created recently, a junior high school.

Michael graduated from Tresco High School in 1942. His brothers had already joined the U.S. Navy and were getting ready to leave for basic training. Michael's teachers had encouraged him to enroll in college, specifically a normal school to become a teacher, which Michael had considered. Instead he joined the U.S. Air Force and put his educational plans on hold.

Michael spent the majority of his time as a gunner in the nose of a B-17 Flying Fortress in the South Pacific. He met up with his brothers a few times near the end of the war and wrote a letter once a week to his mother and sister. Michael and his brothers all spent some time in California on their way to the Pacific Theater. They discussed moving there after the war was over, moving their folks where there was no snow and their dad could find work that was less dangerous.

Michael and his family put what they could into two cars and headed west. They knew that airplane factories in the Los Angeles area were shifting from building war planes to civilian airliners. Michael used his G.I. Bill to purchase a four-unit apartment in suburban Los Angeles. He retrieved his transcripts from Tresco High School and enrolled as a biology major at a local university. Fortunately, the university was close to the factory that assembled parts for airplanes and he was able to get on the night shift. His well-paying job, his hard-earned college degree, and his apartment investment allowed Michael's children opportunities that he had dreamed for them.

Daniel, Michael's eldest son, followed in his father's footsteps and attended the same local university, landed a job in aerospace, and joined the same fraternal organizations as his father. By the late 1970s, he and his wife bought a small home in a fast-growing suburb of Los Angeles that had a reputation for good schools. They were pleased when their daughter, Emilia, expressed interest in becoming a teacher.

Michael's granddaughter, Emilia, now teaches at Pine Hills High School with students from families such as her grandfather's. Emilia loves teaching and loves working with the students at Pine Hills High. She is well aware that she is only one generation removed from the type of poverty that her students now live in. It is her mission to marshal the necessary human and fiscal resources necessary to see that Pine Hills High students acquire the knowledge and skills necessary to fully participate in a democratic society.

Charles

Charles's parents were married in a religious ceremony at their church near a creek in Dothan, Alabama. They called it a church but there were no buildings, only some logs neatly arranged in front of a makeshift altar. The modest church structure served the small Alabama community in every way. The wedding photograph shows Charles's father in a suit that appeared to belong to someone else but the look on his mother's face was captivating. She looked radiant. Her eyes were bright. Charles understood when someone told him that the eyes were the windows to the soul because he had that picture of his parents in his mind's eye.

Charles attended one of the many single-teacher, or one-room schools as they were called in the United States. One woman hired by the township was the teacher of all children, ages 5–17. Charles was a good writer, like his mother, but what he enjoyed most was working with his father fixing machines in the afternoons and on weekends. He was able to see how a machine was put together, how it worked, and what was needed to get it working again. His father said he had a gift for working with his hands. Charles had been in the school now for 10 years. He was occasionally asked to work with students who didn't write as well as he did. He was happy to help, because he considered helping others one of his gifts.

Charles graduated high school and joined his father as the master mechanic of Houston County. He had been thinking about joining the Army for some time but knew that his father would be against the idea for reasons that made sense. Though there were many good reasons to stay, he was confident enlisting in the U.S. Army was the right thing to do.

It became clear to Army officers that the best contribution Charles could make was as a mechanic. At first he was assigned to the motor pool and was dispatched to England fixing anything that could, or couldn't, roll into the maintenance barn. He wrote to his mother and father almost daily. He also began to write about his experiences thinking that some day he just might find someone interested in publishing his stories about the war. As the allied troops moved into Europe, so did Charles. He moved south through France, made it to North Africa for a while, and at the war's end was in charge of a unit in Berlin, repairing the mechanical infrastructure of the city, generators, pumps, and electrical systems.

Charles had decided not to return to Dothan. He didn't see much of a future for himself going back to fixing washers and cars. He had gained experience engineering large systems that ran a major European city. As he thought about places that were growing, he thought that Los Angeles would be a good place for him.

Charles tried to get his parents to move to Los Angeles, but they just didn't see the point in it. Charles had the G.I. Bill so he could get into a house and start working on a college degree. When Charles arrived in Los Angeles, it became clear that he wasn't going to be able to live just anywhere in Los Angeles. There were places where "colored folks" weren't allowed to rent or buy houses. When Charles found a place where he could afford to live he found that the G.I. Bill wouldn't guarantee the loan on a house that was in an area where there were a lot of African Americans.[1] He rented an apartment in southern Los Angeles and focused on getting into college. As he couldn't produce transcripts from that one-room schoolhouse, getting into a four-year college to study engineering wasn't possible; so, he enrolled in the local trade technical college where he took courses in English, mathematics, science, and history. What he found was that the mathematics he had intuited in Berlin and the Army now had to be written out. He hadn't been taught the higher-level math at school and found it more and more difficult to keep up and pursue a degree in engineering.

Charles's son, Raymond, inherited the family interest in mathematics but fell under the influence of what his parents called undesirable friends and didn't apply himself well in high school. He graduated from Pine Hills High School, was in the U.S. Army for two years, and worked at mostly low-wage jobs. To make ends meet, he worked a full-time job at the regional airport and a second job with a maintenance firm. The light of his and his wife's lives was their eldest son, Darren, who they wanted to have opportunities they didn't believe were open to them.

Charles's grandson, Darren, is at Pine Hills High, the same school Charles attended, and has continued to live in the same neighborhood. The school was recently identified as under-performing by the state of

California. Darren is smart but not challenged in school. He likes sports, video games, and anything related to science. He gets by in school because he is perceptive, not because his teachers challenge him.

James Robert

James Robert was a man of the soil. Raised in the hardscrabble hills of eastern Tennessee, he and his young wife moved to Missouri, Colorado, and, finally, to an area in rural southern California. Their moves were always motivated by the promise of job opportunities. James Robert had only rudimentary formal schooling but was well schooled in the prevalent farm duties of the day. The move to southern California resulted in his first permanent job, which was with a large commercial dairy that served small-and mid-sized towns in the area. He and his wife raised nine children, one of whom completed high school.

Though James Robert knew the value of formal education, most of his children left school to find jobs to sustain themselves and the larger family. The men entered the military and served during World War II and the Korean War. The women married in their late teens and early twenties and started families of their own. By modern conventions, today their lives would be described as being working poor. Their fiscal means could not withstand long periods of unemployment. It was the dynamic of living pay check to pay check that seemed to motivate many to leave school after the eighth grade to enter the world of work.

Of James Robert's nine children, only one, his daughter Mary Edith, finished high school. His daughters married young and began families of their own and became homemakers. The sons and sons-in-law, after stints in the military, returned to their hometown and took jobs in local blue-collar industries. By all measures, both generations were leading lives sufficient to provide good homes and adequate sustenance.

Like James Robert, most of the family resided in one area of the community populated by others like them who had migrated from Appalachian regions of the United States. They were served by two elementary schools and, like their parents, most entered but did not finish high school. There were a few of this third generation who did finish high school and go on to college; however, most of this third generation moved to other regions of the country and did not maintain close ties with their families or their hometown.

James Robert's daughter, Mary Edith, and son-in-law had moved closer to Los Angeles to take advantage of job opportunities. The neighborhood had been a stable, blue-collar community when they moved there in the 1950s, but the decline of the aerospace industry combined with the high rate of immigration, mostly from Mexico, caused the family to move to a more distant suburb. The schools were adequate but not known for exemplary academic accomplishments.

Mary Edith had become the caretaker of her granddaughter, Tina, who is attending Pine Hills High School, the same school Mary Edith attended in the 1950s. Tina is a bright, energetic student who seems listless in school. Teachers like her because she is mannerly and causes no disruptions in class.

Teresa

Teresa and her husband entered the United States in the 1910s, following the Mexican Revolution, desperate for work. They had one small child. The decade of the 1910s was particularly difficult in Mexico, and it was easy for their family of three to cross into El Paso and find gainful employment. They had been farmers in Coahuila, and the prospect of working in the fields of southwest Texas was appealing. It was their plan to work long enough to buy a small plot of land in their home state where, in a few years, they could build a life for what they hoped to be a growing family.

In Coahuila they had planned to enroll their son in school, but now that they were in Texas they were not willing to risk being identified as noncitizens of the United States. Both Teresa and her husband had basic literacy skills and knew that they could teach their child enough so that when they returned to Coahuila, he would be able to enter school and catch up in due time. Since they planned to be farmers, they planned for each of their children to attend grammar school.

World War II caused such a drain on the manual labor workforce that in 1942 the U.S. and Mexican governments signed an agreement to create the Bracero Program that resulted in 4,000,000 Mexican workers being brought to work in the fields and markets of the United States. Teresa's husband crossed back and forth across the border during peak harvest times and returned home to his family as opportunities arose. He didn't see a future for his family in the United States and wanted to be able to earn enough to raise his family in the comfort of his beloved Saltillo.

Teresa continued to create a stable home environment for her growing family and ensured that each child was enrolled in school. She and the older children maintained their small farm on which they tended goats and chickens, and maintained a vegetable garden, all of which provided for their basic needs.

Teresa and her family crossed back and forth between Mexico and the United States, wanting to be with the extended family in Coahuila and also earning the higher wages offered in the United States. Teresa's daughter, Guadalupe, was born in Saltillo, Coahuila, Mexico, and was raised in suburban Los Angeles. As a young adult, Guadalupe returned to Saltillo to marry. She and her husband found that to make a living they must migrate to the United States with their family. The family hated leaving the beautiful environs of Coahuila, but the corporatization of Mexican farms made jobs scarce and companies were advertising throughout Mexico for well-paying jobs in the United States.

Guadalupe and her husband, like her grandparents and parents, spoke limited English. They were able to rent apartments in lower-income neighborhoods. They arrived after the passage of California's Proposition 187, with bilingual education being a controversial issue in schools. Pine Hills High School had been declared under-performing by the state of California in response to the emergent accountability movement. In addition to the school serving primarily an English-learning population, 90 percent of the students were eligible for the free and reduced-price lunch program, an indication of a low-income neighborhood. The well-paying jobs that her husband sought did not materialize. After several months as a day laborer, he was able to get a regular job with a residential landscaping firm. Though the job was regular, the pay was modest, and the working hours long.

Guadalupe's son, Alberto, is an average student who likes school, in particular the art program. He is good with freehand drawing, and his art instructor says he has a knack for color and form.

Genealogy of the Four Families

Table 2.4 displays the three generations of Michael, Charles, James Robert, and Teresa's families aligned with prominent historical and educational events of each era. Take a moment and study the table to become acquainted with the four families and to know the manner in which education continues to be an unfolding part of our national histories.

Reflection

In this chapter, historical and educational events that have defined the changing face of public education for the past century were described. Following the description of the events was a description of the experiences of four families, each of which has experienced low-income or impoverished status. Table 2.4 summarizes three generations of four

Table 2.4 Genealogy

	1910s	1920s	1930s	1940s	1950s	1960s	1970s	1980s	1990s	2000s
Historical and Education Events	• 19th amendment provides women voting • Schools segregated throughout U.S. • Compulsory school attendance laws vary among states		• Worldwide economic depression rages • World War II engulfs the U.S. • G.I. Bill provides education benefits		• *Brown* decision ends legal segregation in schools • Civil Rights Act of 1964 enacted • ESEA Title I enacted in 1965		• NAEP begins documenting achievement gap in 1971		• Several states enact accountability measures • NCLB signed 2002	
Michael	Michael enters 1st grade		Michael joins U.S. Air Force and serves as a tail gunner		Michael and family move to suburban Los Angeles		**Daniel's** daughter aspires to be a teacher		**Emilia,** Michael's granddaughter, teaches at Pine Hills High School	
Charles	Charles is in elementary school		Charles joins U.S. Army and is given low-level assignment		Charles and family move to Los Angeles		**Raymond** attends Pine Hills High School		**Darren,** Charles's grandson, attends Pine Hills High School	
James Robert	James Robert completes a couple grades of elementary school		James Robert and family migrate to southern California		James Robert works as an unskilled laborer		**Mary Edith,** James Roberts's daughter, attends Pine Hills High School		**Tina,** Mary Edith's daughter, attends Pine Hills High School	
Teresa	Teresa and husband migrate from Mexico		Teresa works as field hand in Bracero Program		Teresa migrates between Mexico and the U.S.		**Guadalupe,** Teresa's daughter, attends Pine Hills High School		**Alberto,** Guadalupe's son, attends Pine Hills High School	

families alongside pertinent historical and educational events. What observations do you make? What questions surface for you?

_____

_____

_____

_____

Schools as Middle Class Entities: "Saving the Poor"

Howley, Howley, Howley, and Howley (2006), in their remarkable monograph, describe four ways rural schools interact with parents. The Howleys describe these four ways as efforts to "save the poor" (p. 7). We find their descriptions most likely apply to schools throughout Canada and the United States serving parents from low-income communities by rendering them as incapable of knowing and pursuing their own self-interests. The Howleys characterize how middle class schools regard the low-income communities in the following ways:

In Loco Parentis

This approach regards parents as being of limited capability due to the day-to-day struggle in providing for the basic needs of their families and to the parents' own limited education. When educators assume the role of parent and make decisions independently of parents or guardians, and in what educators believe is in the best needs of students they have, educators have wittingly or not put the school in conflict with families of some students. This approach to "saving the poor" is education being viewed as middle class knowledge to be transmitted to the less fortunate (Kovel, 1984; Freire, 1998). Lawson (2003) refers to schools being "school-centric" rather than "community-centric."

Teaching Middle Class Behavior

Comportment is the word of the day for this approach to "saving the poor." If students know how to conduct themselves in a polite manner, they won't embarrass themselves or, more important, those of us in schools. In rural schools, this often entails helping students not appear to be so "country" or behaving like "hicks." Metropolitan schools that embrace this approach want to have students "not be so loud" and to "use proper English."

Extolling the Value of a College Degree

Educators who manifest this perspective often regard parents as not valuing education through perceived nonsupport of the school's efforts to interest their child in a college degree. Too often this approach is expressed in terms of how much more money can be made and, by implication, how the students will enjoy a better life than their parents. How much more effective it would be to interest students in an education for the purpose of controlling their own destinies and being able to right the wrongs being committed in their own communities, which would, of course, often upset the balance of power in many communities (Freire, 1998).

"Othering" the Poor

Kovel (1984) uses the term *thingification* to describe how members of the dominant group use language to distance themselves from others. Lindsey, Nuri-Robins, and Terrell (2009) have identified words used in everyday language by educators that, when used to objectify a group of people, lead to implied and unspoken concepts that function to benefit the dominant group. For instance, when one group of people is referred to as "inferior," by implication the dominant group is implied to be "superior" and the word never has to be spoken.

It is important to note that the Howleys (2006) observe that schools, being the complex systems they are, manifest characterizations of "saving the poor" by being intertwined in the social class stories of schools.

Cultural Proficiency as an Asset-Based Approach

In stark contrast to "saving the poor," cultural proficiency approaches working within low-income communities with the recognition that everyone who enters the school— parent and student alike—brings with them experiences that serve as the foundation for continued learning.

Chapter 3 introduces the tools of cultural proficiency. In the chapter you will learn:

- "Saving the poor" perspectives reflect our personal and institutional barriers to being effective in serving low-income communities.

- The guiding principles for cultural proficiency are a set of core values to guide our work in service of low-income communities, as opposed to changing them.
- The cultural proficiency continuum is a tool to identify our unhealthy and healthy values, language, policies, and practices. You will see efforts to "save the poor" are located on the unhealthy side of the continuum.
- The essential elements function as standards by which we develop effective values, behaviors, policies, and practices.

Going Deeper

Who are Emilia, Darren, Tina, and Alberto in your school? How do you know them? In what ways do you interact with them and their families?

_____

_____

_____

_____

_____

_____

_____

Note

1. Redlining, introduced into public policies of the 1930s, eliminated certain neighborhoods, sometimes based on racial make-up, from consideration for guaranteed loans. Decades later the disparity between the net worth of African Americans nationally was 10 percent of white America (Katznelson, 2005).

3

The Cultural Proficiency Tools Build on Assets

Coming to understand something in a new way can leave us with no choice but to change our lives, including our professional lives, in response. . . . What we cannot do, however, is to pull ourselves out of the equation.

—Sue Books (2004, p. 13)

Getting Centered

Have you heard fellow educators make unhealthy statements such as those that follow and were not sure how to respond? While reading the comments, think of what you would like to say to the speaker:

- "What can you expect from kids who come from homes in *that* neighborhood?"
- "I know race and ethnicity are highly correlated with low achievement, but I still believe poverty is what keeps these kids down!"

Authors' Note: Material in this chapter is derived from two Cultural Proficiency books: Raymond D. Terrell and Randall B. Lindsey, *Culturally Proficient Leadership: The Personal Journey Begins Within,* (2009); and Franklin CampbellJones, Brenda CampbellJones, and Randall B. Lindsey, *The Cultural Proficiency Journey: Moving Beyond Ethical Boundaries Toward Profound School Change,* (2010), both published by Corwin, Thousand Oaks, CA.

- "I just don't think it fair to push the kids too much. The poor dears are doing all they can to survive, and there is no need of my adding to their misery."
- "All I want to do is put in a couple of years here to establish my seniority, and then I am transferring to a school where kids come to school prepared to learn."

When you hear fellow educators talking about students at your school in ways that are unhealthy and you don't say anything, what do you say or wish you had said? Likewise, what does it sound like when fellow educators are engaged in healthy conversation about their practice? Please write your responses to these questions in the space below:

_____

_____

_____

_____

This chapter presents the tools of cultural proficiency as a lens for educators wanting to increase their effectiveness when working with students, parents/guardians, and other members of low-income and impoverished communities. In this chapter you will find the following:

- "Saving the poor" perspectives reflect our personal and institutional barriers to being effective in serving low-income and impoverished communities.
- The Guiding Principles for Cultural Proficiency are a set of core values to guide our work in service of low-income and impoverished communities, as opposed to changing them.
- The Cultural Proficiency Continuum is a tool to identify our unhealthy and healthy values, language, policies, and practices. You will see efforts to "save the poor" are located on the unhealthy side of the continuum.
- The Essential Elements of Cultural Competence function as standards by which we develop effective values, behaviors, policies, and practices.
- Three features of our roles as educators, when embraced intentionally, can foster resiliency in our students.

We, as the authors of this book, call educators together to understand that poverty is not the problem; rather, it is a symptom of social and economic inequities (Books, 2004). Cultural Proficiency provides a perspective and set of tools for how we can maximize our effectiveness in supporting members of low-income and impoverished communities create their own lives in a democratic society. In calling us together, these are our assumptions:

- First, and most important, poverty is *not* a culture. Gorski (2008) traces the origins of the phrase back to Oscar Lewis's *The Children of Sanchez (1961)* and cites extensive empirical research to indicate that the concept of "culture of poverty" is rooted in false stereotypes such as poor work ethic, linguistically deficient, and high rates of alcohol and drug use. Gorski concedes that the use of such stereotypes leads to a culture of classism in how people from impoverished communities are too often viewed.

- Second, poverty is an indicator of socioeconomic disparities that result in children often who are another generation born into poverty, live in more crowded conditions, have parents in low-wage jobs, have less access to enriching cultural experiences, and are in schools with a higher proportion of less-well-prepared teachers than do their counterparts in middle socioeconomic communities (Books, 2004; Rothstein, 2008).

- Third, we must acknowledge that educational gaps are historical, often generational, and persistent. These gaps were in our schools when we arrived, we inherited them, *but we may not ignore them.* The issue of the academic underperformance of children of poverty is an equity issue too long ignored.

- Fourth, if the gaps are to be closed, as well-intentioned and well-informed educators and laypersons, we must step forward as leaders to examine our values and behaviors and the policies and practices of our schools. While we may not be able to solve the socioeconomic disparities of class within our country, we do have the moral responsibility to believe in our students, make certain they understand our belief in their capacity to learn, and militate within our schools and districts for an equitable distribution of resources in terms of well-prepared educators.

- Fifth, we can make a difference for our students and their communities when we listen to who our students say they are and what their needs are. Too often our needs or the needs of the school system take precedent over the needs of our students and their communities.

With these assumptions in mind, you are fully prepared to explore cultural proficiency as a set of tools (the conceptual framework for cultural proficiency is presented in Resource A) to serve you as a responsible person in society, as an effective educator, and as a leader to other educators. In this chapter, we present the tools of cultural proficiency for you to understand yourself as a formal or non-formal leader and your school as an organizational culture in service of students from impoverished conditions.

In this chapter we introduce cultural proficiency as

- A process that begins with us, not with our students or their communities
- A shift in thinking for some educators that moves us from viewing children of poverty as problematic to embracing and esteeming their capacity to learn
- A lens through which we view our role as educators
- Being comprised of a set of four interrelated tools to guide our practice

Building on Other's Assets: Cultural Proficiency's Inside-Out Process

Cross et al. (1989) to cultural proficiency being an inside-out process of personal and organizational change. Cultural proficiency is who we are, more than what we do. Effective use of the tools of cultural proficiency is predicated on your ability and willingness to recognize that change is an inside-out process in which we are students of our assumptions about self, others, and the context in which we work with others. It is our intent to guide you in this book in such a way that you will reflect on your actions, the actions of your school, and the cultural communities you serve. This book engages your leadership journey with many activities that have the following in common:

- You will recognize your own assumptions and retain those that facilitate culturally proficient actions and change those that impede such actions.
- You will apply this inside-out process to examine and change as appropriate school policies and practices that either impede or facilitate cultural proficient ends.

The willingness and ability to examine yourself and your school is fundamental to addressing educational gap issues. Cultural proficiency provides a comprehensive, systemic structure for school leaders to identify, examine, and discuss educational issues in our schools. The four tools of cultural proficiency provide the means to assess and change your values and behaviors and your school's policies and practices in ways that serve our students, schools, communities, and society. Your educational journey using cultural proficiency as a means for self-growth begins with mastery of the four tools of cultural proficiency as a philosophical imperative.

Cultural Proficiency Represents a Paradigm Shift for Viewing Poverty

Cultural proficiency is a mindset for how we interact with all people, irrespective of their cultural or demographic memberships. Cultural proficiency is a worldview that carries explicit values, language, and standards for effective personal interactions and professional practices. Cultural proficiency is a 24/7 approach to our personal and professional lives. Most important, cultural proficiency is *not* a set of independent activities or strategies that you learn to use with others—your students, colleagues, or community members.

Too often, we meet and work with educators looking for shortcuts to working with people who live in impoverished conditions. It is our experience that educators seeking shortcuts to working in cross-cultural settings have an innate belief in their own superiority and view others as needing to be changed. To address such shortcomings, Cross et al. (1989) was motivated to develop cultural competence and cultural proficiency when he recognized that mental health professionals and institutions often were ineffective in cross-cultural settings.

Educators who commit to culturally proficient practices represent a paradigmatic shift away from the current, dominant group view of regarding "underperforming" groups of students from poverty as problematic. Take a few moments and study Table 3.1, the Cultural Proficiency Continuum. Note that the use of the term "tolerance" is associated with Cultural Destructiveness, Cultural Incapacity, and Cultural Blindness, while "transformation" is associated with Cultural Precompetence, Cultural Competence, and Cultural Proficiency. In terms of this book, the shift from "tolerance" to "transformation" is paradigmatic. In the lives of our students, the monumental shift is from us educators holding a value of "tolerating children of poverty" to our holding a "transformational commitment to equity without regard to students' social class." The students remain the same, the shift is in our approach to how we approach working with our students.

Table 3.1   The Cultural Proficiency Continuum

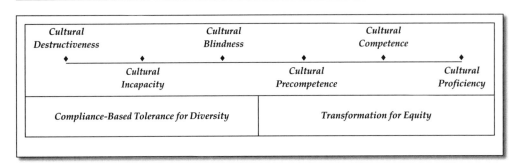

Source: Adapted from Raymond D. Terrell and Randall B. Lindsey (2009), *Culturally Proficient Leadership: The Personal Journey Begins Within.* Thousand Oaks, CA: Corwin.

Representative comments from the "tolerance" paradigm are *Poor people don't value education; They just need to work harder; It isn't about race it is about socioeconomic status;* and *They just need to pull themselves up by their bootstraps—millions of immigrants have succeeded; my ancestors did!*

In contrast, culturally proficient educators hold a "transformational" paradigm that views their work in terms of how they, the educator, affects the educational experiences of people from impoverished backgrounds. Transformational comments are *What do we need to learn to be effective? What might be instructional approaches that work in this setting? How can our educator groups advocate for equitable distribution of resources to schools in greatest need?* and *In what ways can I organize the agenda to focus on being solution-centered?*

Cultural Proficiency as a Lens

Culturally proficient educators are effective working with students from low-income and impoverished communities, the adults in the communities they serve, and the educators and staff members in their schools. Culturally proficient educators are committed to educating all students to high levels through knowing, valuing, and using the students' cultural backgrounds, languages, and learning styles within the selected curricular and instructional contexts. Leaders who are committed to leading our schools in a way that all students have access to the benefits of a democratic system can use the four tools of cultural proficiency as a template for their personal and professional development.

The Cultural Proficiency Tools

The tables in the pages that follow portray the tools of cultural proficiency as interrelated and interdependent. The tools of cultural proficiency provide you with

- *Barriers* to this work framed in such a way that you avoid "saving the poor perspectives" in favor of intentional use of the guiding principles and essential elements;
- *Guiding principles* on which you can build an ethical and professional frame for effective communication and problem solving to guide our work in service of people in low-income communities, as opposed to trying to change them;
- A *continuum* of behaviors that enables you to diagnose your own unhealthy and healthy values and behaviors in such a way that you can better influence the policies and practices of our profession; and,
- *Essential elements* expressed in terms of standards of personal and professional conduct that serve as a framework for intentionally responding to the academic and social needs of the varied groups in your school and community.

Effective use of these tools is predicated on a willingness to recognize the assumptions within you and your school described above. The examination of assumptions begins with you the educator, not with your colleagues. It is our experience that effective educators are very clear about themselves relative to working with and leading diverse communities.

Cultural proficiency is an interrelated set of four tools that prompt reflection and provide the opportunity to improve your leadership practice in service of others. The tools provide you with the means by which to lead your personal life and perform your professional responsibilities in a culturally proficient manner.

The Guiding Principles and the Barriers to Cultural Proficiency

The Guiding Principles of Cultural Proficiency provide a moral response for overcoming the barriers to cultural proficiency. There is a recognizable disconnect between the guiding principles of cultural proficiency and the barriers to cultural proficiency as reflected in educators' *values* and schools' *policies*. Addressing this disconnect is an important step to identifying and clarifying educators' and schools' core values in providing educational opportunities for all socioeconomic groups of students.

Table 3.2 presents the Barriers to Cultural Proficiency in the column to the left and the Guiding Principles to Cultural Proficiency in the column to the right. You will notice a narrow, center column that contains the solitary word "versus," which denotes the divide between acknowledging the barriers and making a commitment to overcoming the barriers.

Table 3.2   The Barriers to Cultural Proficiency Versus the Guiding Principles

The Barriers to Cultural Proficiency	versus	The Guiding Principles
• Resistance to change; viewing change as needing to be done by others, not by one's self • Systems of oppression; acknowledging and recognizing that classism, racism, sexism, ethnocentrism, and other forms of oppression are real experiences • A sense of privilege and entitlement; unawareness or indifference to benefits that accrue solely by one's membership in a social class, gender, racial, or other cultural group		• Culture is a predominant force in people's and school's lives • People are served in varying degrees by the dominant culture • People have group identities and individual identities • Diversity within cultures is vast and significant • Each cultural group has unique cultural needs • The best of both worlds enhances the capacity of all • The family, as defined by each culture, is the primary system of support in the education of children • School systems must recognize that marginalized populations have to be at least bicultural and that this status creates a unique set of issues to which the system must be equipped to respond • Inherent in cross-cultural interactions are dynamics that must be acknowledged, adjusted to, and accepted

Reflection

Take a moment and read the words in the first column of Table 3.2. As you read the terms and phrases in the first column, what feelings, reactions, or thoughts occur to you? Please record your responses in the space below.

_____

_____

_____

_____

For many people, the words and phrases will appear scary and/ or irritating. Some readers may respond with feeling blamed, angry, guilty, depressed, or with questions such as "but, where do we go from here?" Other readers may respond by feeling validated, curious, and with questions such as "yes, so this is my reality and what are we going to do about it?"

This book is dedicated to bringing us together in dialogue with the Guiding Principles of Cultural Proficiency as the common ground for discussion. To have dialogue about the guiding principles begins with recognizing the barriers are real for many people while for others the barriers may be invisible or not recognizable. To enter into dialogue about the barriers and responsibility for addressing them is to be aware of the emotional baggage that exists on both sides of the issue and to be committed to a shared moral commitment of providing equitable educational opportunities to all socioeconomic groups of students in our communities.

As you can see, we present the Guiding Principles of Cultural Proficiency as a countermeasure to the barriers and the means to develop a moral frame for recognizing right from wrong and to pursue just means in educating all children in our schools to high levels. The barriers represent the intractable issues that have historically stymied, and continue to stymie to this day, broad-scale school reform intended to provide adequate and appropriate education to historically underserved cultural groups of students.

Our resistance to change as educators is historical and is embodied in two highly observable ways. First, every two years since 1971 the National Association of Educational Progress (Perie et al., 2005) has documented, and circulated widely in the education community, detailed descriptions of academic achievement gaps. Second, in spite of the NAEP data being very public, it has taken state and national education reforms, most widely evident in the federal reauthorization of ESEA Title I's No Child Left Behind Act (2002), to set targets for academic achievement in order to hold educators accountable. The continuing presence of educational gaps is a challenge to those of us at all levels in the education community to examine why education and academic achievement gaps continue to persist among demographic groups of our students. As a profession, we have acted as if the NAEP data has not existed. We struggle in addressing the inequities so well documented in the data.

Resistance to changing educational practice is tied to the intractability of historical systems of oppression such as classism, racism, ethnocentrism, sexism, and heterosexism. Your response to the reflection activity above most likely serves as an indicator to levels of discomfort in dealing with these issues. Can you guess how your educator colleagues would respond to the words in the first column of Table 3.2? That is where the dialogue must take place—with and among our colleagues.

The Guiding Principles of Cultural Proficiency provide educators with an inclusive worldview that embraces Freire's (1987) maxim that there is no teaching without learning (p. 56). The guiding principles are a moral frame to examine the biannual NAEP reports and other similar data and to conclude that current educational practices are not equitable. Accordingly, we recognize that some students are well served by current policies and practices. Unfortunately, recognizing that current practices serve some well often leads to a sense of entitlement and privilege that causes those well served to turn a blind eye to those not well served. It is the dynamic tension between who is well served and who is underserved that leads us into dialogue and to embrace the moral foundation of the Guiding Principles of Cultural Proficiency as a framework for serving the educational needs of all our students.

Highly evolved moral development characterizes educators and other persons who hold principled perspectives and who transcend prevailing norms to serve the underserved (CampbellJones, 2002). Evolved senses of justice and fairness lead to using the Guiding Principles of Cultural Proficiency as ethical maxims and the Continuum and Five Essential Elements as behavioral guidelines for educators and school systems alike.

The Guiding Principles of Cultural Proficiency as represented in Table 3.2 provide guidance for educators' values and behaviors and for the development of schools' policies and practices. Embracing these principles as foundational to our work with students, parents/guardians, and members of low-income and impoverished communities is foundational to progress. Adherence to the guiding principles makes transition to the "healthy" side of the Continuum and the ability to employ use of the Essential Elements of Cultural Competence as standards for personal conduct and school practices.

The Continuum and the Essential Elements

The Cultural Proficiency Continuum and the Five Essential Elements of Cultural Competence provide a template for the *behaviors* of educators and the *practices* of schools. The continuum and elements build on the moral frame of the guiding principles and provide an ethical base from which to make professional choices:

- The continuum describes unhealthy and healthy values and behaviors of educators and policies and practices of schools; in other words, a moral distinction between unfair and wrong to the left side of the continuum (i.e., destructiveness, incapacity, blindness) and fair and just to the right side of the continuum (i.e., precompetence, competence, proficiency).

- The essential elements provide standards for educators and schools; in other words, the alignment of ethical principles with educator behaviors and school practices.

Table 3.3 describes the six points of the continuum. Take a moment to read Table 3.3 and note the "action words" on each side of the

Table 3.3 The Cultural Proficiency Continuum: Depicting Unhealthy and Healthy Practices

Cultural Destructiveness ◆ *Cultural Incapacity* ◆	*Cultural Blindness* ◆ *Cultural Precompetence* ◆	*Cultural Competence* ◆ *Cultural Proficiency* ◆
Compliance-Based Tolerance for Diversity	*Transformation for Equity*	
• *Cultural Destructiveness.* Seeking to eliminate references to the socioeconomics of "others" in all aspects of the school and in relationship with their communities. • *Cultural Incapacity.* Trivializing other cultures and socioeconomic status and seeking to make them appear to be wrong. • *Cultural Blindness.* Pretending not to see or acknowledge the socioeconomic status and culture of others and choosing to ignore the experiences of such groups within the school and community.	• *Cultural Precompetence.* Increasingly aware of what you and the school don't know about working in diverse settings. It is at this key level of development that you and the school can move in a positive, constructive direction or you can vacillate, stop, and possibly regress. • *Cultural Competence.* Manifesting your personal values and behaviors and the school's policies and practices in a manner that is inclusive with cultures and socioeconomic communities that are new or different from you and the school. • *Cultural Proficiency.* Advocating for lifelong learning for the purpose of being increasingly effective in serving the educational needs of the socioeconomic and cultural groups served by the school. Holding the vision that you and the school are instruments for creating a socially just democracy.	

Source: Adapted from Raymond D. Terrell and Randall B. Lindsey (2009), *Culturally Proficient Leadership: The Personal Journey Begins Within.* Thousand Oaks, CA: Corwin.

continuum. Behaviors and practices located on the left side of the continuum (i.e., destructiveness, incapacity, blindness) give evidence of "barriers." Behaviors and practices on the right side of the continuum (i.e., precompetence, competence, proficiency), specifically those regarded as culturally competent and proficient, reflect commitment to the guiding principles as educators' and schools' moral bearing and reliance on the guiding principles as ethical assumptions.

Reflection

Now that you have studied the continuum, what are your thoughts and reactions? Where do you see yourself relative to the students of poverty in your school? Where do you see your school along the continuum? Can you identify practices in your school at each point of the continuum? Please use the space below to record your responses.

_____

_____

_____

_____

The continuum should make clear the moral vision of educating all students to high levels. Most of us want our educational practice to be on the right side of the continuum and, most likely, don't know how to get there and may not have the resolve to ask the difficult, courageous questions of *Why are our students of poverty not achieving?* and *What is in our power to reverse that trend?* "Nothing" is not an acceptable response.

Once the moral resolve of asking the difficult questions of our colleagues and ourselves has been put on the table and the guiding principles are acknowledged as an ethical framework, the Five Essential Elements of Cultural Competence serve as standards for individual educators and schools alike. These five elements become the standards to which we measure the efficacy of our curriculum, the effectiveness of instructional strategies, the relevance of professional development, the utility of systems of assessment and accountability, and the intent of parent and community communications and outreach.

Table 3.4 contains concise descriptions of the Five Essential Elements. Please note the empowering language of learning that is part of each element and that each element serves as a standard for professional behavior and schoolwide practices.

Table 3.4 The Essential Elements for Culturally Proficient Practices

- *Assessing Cultural Knowledge.* Learning about the community you serve, about how educators and the school as a whole react to the community you serve, and what you need to do to be effective in low-income and impoverished communities. Also, leading for learning about the school and its grade levels and departments as cultural entities in responding to the educational needs of the community.
- *Valuing Diversity.* Creating informal and formal decision-making groups inclusive of parents/guardians and community members whose viewpoints and experiences are different from yours and those of the dominant group at the school, and that will enrich conversations, decision making, and problem solving.
- *Managing the Dynamics of Difference.* Modeling problem solving and conflict resolution strategies as a natural and normal process within the culture of the schools and the socioeconomic contexts of the communities of your school.
- *Adapting to Diversity.* Learning about socioeconomic and cultural groups different from your own and the ability to use others' experiences and backgrounds in all school settings.
- *Institutionalizing Cultural Knowledge.* Making learning about socioeconomic and cultural groups and their experiences and perspectives an integral part of the school's professional development.

Source: Adapted from Raymond D. Terrell and Randall B. Lindsey (2009), *Culturally Proficient Leadership: The Personal Journey Begins Within.* Thousand Oaks, CA: Corwin.

Reflection

In this chapter, you have proceeded from a description of the barriers to cultural proficiency and have now arrived at a consideration of five standards intended to support you in service of all students in your classrooms and school. How do you react to the essential elements? In what way do the essential elements reflect the ethics in the Guiding Principles of Cultural Proficiency? To what extent do you want these standards to serve your educational practice and that of your school in service of students of poverty? Please use the space below to record your responses.

_____

_____

_____

_____

Please note that the five essential elements exist at the "cultural competence" point of the Continuum. Proficiency is when an educator or school has incorporated the essential elements into their practice to the extent that they develop at least these commitments:

- A commitment to one's own learning as an ongoing, immutable process.
- A commitment to social justice that addresses the educational needs of all current and emerging cultural groups in the school and community.
- A commitment to advocacy that is natural, normal, and effective.
- A commitment to mentoring the underserved to have access to educational opportunity and to mentoring those well served by current practice to become aware of and responsive to underserved individuals and cultural groups. The underserved could be colleagues, students, and/or members of the community.

Therefore, schools serving low-income and impoverished communities have the opportunity to learn from and with members of their communities. Educators view their role to provide the knowledge and skills for members to pursue their own self-interests. In pursuing their own self-interest, students are viewed by educators to be competent and worthy of a high-quality educational experience.

Cultural Proficiency and Resiliency: Educators and Students

Cultural Proficiency aligns with resiliency research in response to working with students from low-income and impoverished communities. Intentional use of the cultural proficiency tools starts a process, which can initiate a reform action that will attack the achievement gap by mitigating poverty as one of the potent factors thwarting children and youth in Canada and the United States.

Three important features of our roles as educators, when embraced intentionally, can foster resiliency within students when low-income and impoverished community status provokes adversity. It is important to note that these three features apply to educators as much as they do to the students with whom we work. How we approach and work successfully with low-income and impoverished communities has three distinguishing features:

Feature 1: Transition From Deficit- to Asset-Based Perspective

One feature is our perspective can heighten or mitigate effects of poverty when poverty provokes adversity for the student, his family, or his relationships at school. Awareness of students' out of school adversity and related needs allows us to advocate through community-based agencies or other problem-solving approaches and thereby empower the students' relationships with others. To achieve this type of relationship with a student necessitates an intentional transition from a deficit perspective to an asset-based approach. Accordingly, for schools to truly be effective, educators must grapple with their own value-laden biases and views that might be interfering with student success. We must examine our assumptions that embrace the deficit perspective, where students are regarded as problems that need to be fixed, to a strength-based approach, where students are experienced as competent, capable, and needing support and resources to realize how to learn best while acknowledging their future-focused goals.

Feature 2: Importance of Influential Adults

A second feature underscores the importance and validity of influential adult relationships in the lives of students affected by poverty and other forms of adversity. Werner and Smith (1982, 1992, & 2001) found that caring, nurturing adults facilitate successful achievement for students. All relationships between students and educators impact youth. Ultimately, achievement relies on supportive, adult relationships to make school work for students from low-income and impoverished communities. Educators are key to constructive youth development when we reach out in an intentional manner and become a positive influence in students' lives beyond the classroom.

Feature 3: Belief That We Humans Are "Self-Righting"

A third feature is embracing a belief and faith in the fact that our students, and we, as educators, are "self-righting" or resilient. Many of the youth we are concerned about today will make choices that will help them change the trajectory of their lives—eventually. We must create the conditions in our schools where low- and non-achieving students experience learning as making choices that affect their lives today and into the future. This becomes a particular challenge when acknowledging that often the school itself is suspect for perpetuating the conditions that have thwarted students' learning. Haberman (2005) describes self-righting when we, as educators, and our students alike recognize the following:

- *We can change our behavior.* There is no permanent "stuck" place for us or for our students. We can recover and change. It is not possible to eradicate the past; it is possible to start something today and change your lives. It is the transformational commitment of human choice.
- *We can shift perceptions or paradigms.* The shift can begin as thinking or as an emotional process that results in behavior and attitudinal changes. The longer a person lives with the Cultural Proficiency lens, the more likely the change will sustain.
- *We can reorganize choices and priorities.* Making decisions to become different must be complemented by the actions that anchor the change. As an analogy, choosing to diet won't make you lose weight. Making the choice coupled with a good food plan and exercise will likely result in weight loss. Prioritizing how you see food and exercise in your life will likely make permanent the change in behavior.
- *We can request help from professionals.* No one has perfect lenses all the time. Sometimes a colleague or other professional is needed to coach us in our change processes.
- *We can resolve conflict and how we act or believe.* Conflict is normal and natural. How we manage conflict can help move a relationship to a higher level and lead to more effective communications. When resolved in real time, conflict will hopefully not become distorted, gather emotional overloading from past injustices, or become a tool to hurt other persons. Resolved conflict can become a tool for intimacy and improved discourse.
- *We can use prosocial responses to stress or problems.* Coping is what an individual does to establish balance in their lives. Balancing does not necessarily mean that a person makes logical or healthy choices. Moderate exercise, good food plans, counseling, group counseling, talking with friends, trying new ways to get needs met, and abstaining are all prosocial responses to stress.
- *We can seek new ways to see the world.* The way we view the world motivates how we respond to it.

Educators who view themselves as "self-righting" are effective teachers who engage students and their students' parents/guardians in ways that acknowledge the potential in each student and engage with students in ways that treat them in all of their potential. Self-righting, or resilient, educators recognize that within the impoverished or low-income conditions of their students exist children and youth who have experiences on which appropriate education can be built. These educators recognize it is their responsibility to learn about the milieu of their students, which is the first step in serving student needs. Knowing students' surroundings and environments is an important step in being able to relate to students and to structure culturally responsive educational experiences.

These three features for working with low-income and impoverished communities allow us to be intentional in developing a culturally proficient asset-based perspective, in being an influential adult in our students' lives, and be "self-righting" in making choices for ourselves and how we work with our students and their families.

Going Deeper

What have you learned in this chapter? What new questions do you now have? Thinking of your role as an educator, how does the information from this chapter cause you to think differently about your practice? How does this information cause you to think differently about your school/district? How does this chapter cause you to think differently about poverty?

_____

_____

_____

_____

_____

_____

_____

_____

PART II

Prosocial School Applications

The chapters in this section focus on Emilia's personal transformation and her efforts to influence and transform the beliefs and practices of her colleagues. Emilia's participation in a professional development session causes her to reflect on her own upbringing in a low-income community and to be ever more aware of students like Alberto, Tina, and Darren. Emilia returns to her classroom viewing her own pedagogy in a way that shapes her approaches to school leadership practices and policymaking. She is convinced that commitment to her students begins in the classroom and must, necessarily, impact the culture of Pine Hills High School. Emilia proceeds from the notion that the inside-out approach to change is both personal and systemic.

The chapters in this section are designed for you to begin with the classroom and move progressively to school-level, community-level, and implications for professional leadership. A core tenet of cultural proficiency is the *inside-out approach* that begins with consideration of your values and behavior and your school's and district's policies and practices. We regard the inside-out process as prosocial in that it describes people with strength of character who exhibit socially just behaviors (Werner & Smith, 1992). People with this strength of character are intentional in moving their own values and behaviors, and the policies and practices of their school, from the "unhealthy" side of the Cultural Proficiency Continuum (please refer to Table 3.3 in Chapter 3) to the "healthy" side of the continuum.

In each chapter you will build an understanding that systemic change begins with personal awareness and is, then, reflected in the policies and practices that you and your colleagues develop and implement at all levels of schooling and the profession of education. Table 1.2, Chapter 1, illustrates how asset-based and deficit-based perspectives of poverty intersect with the Cultural Proficiency Continuum. The column on the left side of the table presents deficit-based perspectives of poverty correlating with Cultural Destructiveness, Incapacity, and Blindness. In sharp contrast, the column to the right presents asset-based perspectives of poverty being aligned with Cultural Precompetence, Competence, and Proficiency.

Chapters 4, 5, and 6 are cumulative in design (Dilts, 1994). Using the information gained in Part I, each subsequent chapter in Part II builds on the knowledge and skills of the preceding chapter to create a systemic spiral of information and skills for educators to use in support of all students learning. Chapter 4 focuses on classroom issues and the role of the teacher. It should be elemental that teaching is the core purpose of schooling. To that end, Chapter 4 holds a value for teaching in such a way that students view themselves as capable of understanding and changing their own world (Freire, 1998; Gutstein, 2007).

Chapter 5 expands our attention to grade-level, department, and schoolwide leadership in support of instruction and learning and holds teaching as the most important adult activity at the school. Culturally proficient leadership focuses on educators exploring and understanding the bases for their assumptions about poverty, the conditions of poverty, and people from impoverished backgrounds. Chapter 6 considers the role of educational leaders as policymakers in responding to parents, guardians, and community issues. Culturally proficient policymakers use the demographics of the community to inform the creation and use of policies and practices designed and implemented to serve current community members.

4

Culturally Proficient Pedagogy

There is no teaching without learning.

—Paulo Freire, 1987, p. 56

Getting Centered

"Poverty and Social Justice"—the title of the weekend retreat intrigued Emilia. Emilia, the granddaughter of Michael whom you met in Chapter 2, is a teacher at Pine Hills High School. She had looked forward to the State Teachers' Association (STA) weekend retreat (the training script for the STA session is Resource B) mostly because its professional development programs are thought provoking and relevant to her as a classroom teacher. But the topic of this retreat had particular relevance. When the presenters posed the following questions at the outset of the meeting, she was taken aback:

- What barriers to student learning exist within our schools and us?
- What are your and your school's core values that support equitable learning outcomes for students?
- What examples do you have for unhealthy and healthy language, behaviors, policies, and practices used by you, your colleagues, and your school?
- What standards do you and your school use to ensure equitable learning outcomes for students?

It has been three days since the retreat and Emilia is still spinning from the answers she had begun to craft to those questions. We ask you to take a moment and put yourself in Emilia's shoes; how might you have responded to those four questions for your school and yourself? Please use the space below to record your response.

_____

_____

_____

_____

Pine Hills High School's Socioeconomic Context

Emilia realized that she had enrolled for the STA professional development session with a naïve expectation—that there was something "about poverty" that she needed to learn to be successful with the students in her school. After all, Pine Hills High School was known as the high school with a preponderance of youth from low-income families. Though the school was ethnically and racially diverse, it was uniform in the socioeconomic status of the students. It was an open secret that many teachers and administrators came to Pine Hills to begin their careers and, when opportunities arose, transferred across town to affluent Maple View High School or to similar schools in neighboring districts.

Emilia's *aha* during the weekend retreat was that learning "about poverty" was only a small part of what was needed for her to be an effective educator. The bigger learning was that her individual perspective, and the school's collective perspective, about people from low-income and impoverished settings contribute to student success. More important, she was confronted with the reality that their perspectives are the one thing educators can control. The session presenters made no attempt to diminish the effect of structural economic inequities that exist within society; rather, they emphasized that what occurred within the walls of our schools is the one part of our students' daily lives over which we have control.

The presenters at the weekend STA professional development made the same connection with Pogrow's (2009) contention as was made in Chapter 1: Children born into poverty are as capable and bright as anyone, and it is our responsibility as educators to find the moral resolve and appropriate strategies to engage students. Emilia learned that between the third and fifth grades, many students from low-income and impoverished communities start choosing alternatives for their attention and energy and school ceases being relevant. Without meaning and relevance, many such students become passive learners (Ferguson, 2007). For Emilia, the weekend provided professional and personal connections. She saw an urgent need to understand the connection between cultural proficiency and working with students from low-income or impoverished communities.

The major link to her profession made by Emilia during the weekend retreat was that she was among a core group of teachers and the principal at Pine Hills High School who were intentional in staying at the school because of their strong commitment to the students. Emilia's personal connection at the retreat was her recognition that she was only one or two generations removed from the poverty that enmeshed her students. She entered the retreat wanting to know more about the conditions of poverty. She left the retreat with lots of information about issues of poverty. Her deeper learning, however, was about herself and questions about the policies and practices of Pine Hills High School with regard to students from low-income or impoverished backgrounds.

Intent of This Chapter

This chapter is for teachers and those who support teachers to reflect on your practice in such a way that you can better serve the social and academic needs of students in your classrooms. Through the use of descriptive information, vignettes, and reflective questions, you will assess the extent to which you may be

- Beginning the *inside-out process* of identifying barriers to learning and core values that support learning within you or your classroom
- Fostering *conditions for learning* within your classroom to support equitable learning opportunities
- Exhibiting a *culturally competent praxis*[1] that organizes instruction to reflect knowledge and appreciation of students' communities

Beginning the Inside-Out Process

We begin by inviting you to think deeply about your approach to instruction (your pedagogy) related to the tools of Cultural Proficiency that were described in Chapter 3. Table 4.1 presents a series of open-ended questions for your thoughtful consideration. Take a few minutes and record your responses to the prompts.

Table 4.1   Beginning the Inside-Out Process

Becoming a culturally proficient educator begins with understanding our own reactions to our students and their communities. This activity is designed to support you in a personal exploration of your views and potential biases. Knowing more about your views and biases equips you to be ever more intentional in your development as an increasingly effective educator.

Please take a few minutes and record your responses to these questions. Be thoughtful and reflective in your responses.

In what ways do you describe your students from low-income or impoverished communities?

_____

_____

In what ways do you describe your students' parents, guardians, or foster care providers?

_____

_____

In what ways do you describe the neighborhoods in which your students live?

_____

_____

In what ways do you describe the language your students speak at home?

_____

_____

In what ways do you describe yourself in relation to the community you serve?

_____

_____

In what ways do you describe your school in relation to the community you serve?

_____

_____

Making Sense of Your Responses

Study your responses in Table 4.1 and look for themes in the adjectives you used. For any *negative* terms or phrases, ask yourself questions such as the following:

- To what extent are you focused on your students' exterior trappings?
- To what extent have you tried to learn your students' interests or surroundings?
- To what extent do you assign blame to parents, guardians, or foster care providers?
- How much do you know about the communities in which your students live? Have you made home visits or visits to local businesses? If so, what judgments might you have made?
- To what extent do you validate your students' bi-literacy? Even if your students are English speakers, to what extent do you recognize they need to be bi-cultural to be successful in school?

For responses that elicit *positive* responses and themes, ask yourself questions such as these:

- To what extent are you able to identify students' assets? What do you know about their interests, preferences, or strengths?
- In what positive ways do you regard the parents, guardians, or foster care providers?
- In what ways can you describe your students' home or community-based support systems? What community challenges exist that impinge on your students?
- How well do you think you could navigate in your students' community? What knowledge and skills do your students possess, that you don't, which enables them to navigate their community?

Reflection

These questions were designed to guide your thinking about barriers to and guiding principles in support of culturally proficient practices. Use the space below to record your responses to the questions and your reaction to the questions.

_____

_____

_____

_____

We Create Conditions for Learning

As educators, we influence our students' lives in many ways. One of those ways is the manner in which we structure our classrooms for teaching and learning, the value we place on formal and non-formal school leadership focused on instruction, and policy development that expects and supports academic and social success for all students that acknowledges and honors their cultural backgrounds. A classroom or school environment can be friendly and welcoming or it can be a foreign, hostile place that communicates a preference for some cultural groups of students and not for others. Efficacious educators respect cultural differences and shared similarities.

An emerging body of work known as "academic optimism" provides guidance by describing key elements in successful elementary and secondary schools with high rates of low-income and impoverished students. Hoy, Tarter, and Hoy's 2006 study was important for two reasons: It presented a comprehensive review of the literature related to student achievement being related to forces within schools, and their study of 96 high schools further demonstrated the presence of academic optimism in schools with low socioeconomic students, parents, and guardians. Their study continued to document the presence of three organizational properties that positively impact student achievement:

- Schools are driven by academic emphases.
- Beliefs of efficacy are present in educators, students, and the school.
- Pervasive trust of students and parents are interrelated.

Hoy et al. (2006) combine these three organizational properties that positively impact student achievement with the traditional view of achievement being a function of talent and motivation, to which they add—"academic optimism." To illustrate academic optimism, they offer this quote from Seligman:

> Seligman argues that learned optimism gets people over the wall of learned pessimism and not just as individuals but also as organizational members. In the same way that individuals can develop learned helplessness, organizations can be seduced by pervasive pessimism. The pessimistic view says, with tired resignation, "These kids can't learn and there is nothing I can do about it, so why worry about academic achievement?" This view is reinforcing, self-fulfilling, and defeating. Academic optimism, in stark contrast, views teachers as capable, students as willing, parents as supportive, and the task as achievable (as cited in Hoy et al., 2006, p. 437).

The combination of organizational properties and academic optimism leads us to the work of Haberman (1995, 2005), who has been a champion for urban educators for over 40 years in his roles as a teacher, principal, trainer, credentialing expert, and researcher. He has studied conditions that support optimal learning in urban, impoverished communities. We find that his work on behalf of urban educators applies to educators, irrespective of local conditions, who are in service of students from low-income or impoverished communities. Haberman (1995) estimates that nearly 3,000 youth drop out daily from schools throughout the United States, and most of them are minority youth from the poorest social classes—African American, Latino, and Southeast Asian students—exacerbating the racial and class gap. He maintains, "The persistent shortage of teachers who can be effective in 120 failing urban school systems guarantees that the mis-education of seven million diverse children in urban poverty will continue" (p. 49).

Haberman studied successful urban teachers of students living in poverty. He organized the teachers into three groups—the "stars," the "quitters," and the "leavers." He found that the stars had remarkably different ways of being and functioning with children and youth living in poverty than those who quit the profession quickly or after a period of effort. The "star" teachers became their students' mentors, guides, and facilitators of learning. He identified seven functions that help to discern effectiveness in urban teachers of the poor:

- *High Expectations.* The demonstrated belief that all of the children can be successful if appropriately taught.
- *Organizational Ability.* The skill to plan, gather materials, and set up a workable classroom.
- *Physical/Emotional Stamina.* The ability to persist with commitment and enthusiasm after instances of violence, death, and other crises.
- *Teaching Style.* The use of coaching rather than direction and information giving.
- *Explanations of Success.* An emphasis on student effort rather than presumed ability.
- *Ownership.* The willingness to lead students to believe it is their classroom, not the teacher's.
- *Inclusion.* The acceptance of accountability for all the students assigned to the classroom.

Pedagogical Preparation: Then and Now

Think about the people we introduced in Chapter 2. Don't you wonder about the educators who might have taught Michael (a first-generation Italian immigrant), Charles (an African American from Alabama), James Robert (an in-country white migrant who moved from eastern Tennessee to California), and Teresa (an immigrant from Mexico)? What kinds of training did their teachers have? Do you suppose there were long discussions about pedagogy and learning styles in a teacher's lounge?

Of course, we don't have information about the teachers of these four people, but we do know that until after World War II it was unlikely that Michael, Charles, James Robert, or Teresa would progress much beyond eighth grade. The world of work required levels of education that were satisfied for most people by the end of eighth grade. Those who proceeded to high school and college represented a small portion of the population.

What we know is post–World War II Canada and the United States ushered in a new era in education. More people were attending high school and college than at any previous period of history. For the first time, the United States set standards to serve low-income and impoverished families through the Elementary and Secondary Education Act's (ESEA) Title I Program (1965) and, inadvertently, defined social class through participation in ESEA's Free and Reduced Lunch Program. Increasingly stringent school attendance laws were enacted that required attendance to age 18 or high school graduation. The newly expanded graduation requirements led to a larger portion of children from low-income backgrounds attending school for longer periods of time.

Recent accountability measures, such as No Child Left Behind (2002) in the United States, are the modern iteration of ESEA. NCLB and similar state and provincial laws have brought attention to the reality that students from low-income and impoverished backgrounds, like students who are African American, Latino, or English learners, are either chronically failing in our schools or are seriously lagging in achievement. The social, economic, and political inequities that create and foster low-income and impoverished communities are exacerbated when lack of access to basic education over two to three generations is coupled with disparate levels of achievement. What had once been known mostly to those affected, people who reside in low-income and impoverished communities and the schools that serve them, is now widely publicized as "the achievement gap." What was once an open secret and perpetuated by not wanting our children to go to "those schools" is now, as it should be, a measure of accountability for our schools and our societies in Canada and the United States. Most important, the achievement gap is more than academic test measurements; it also is comprised of access and opportunity gaps.

In this chapter we are reintroduced to the third generation that followed Michael, Charles, James Robert, and Teresa. Today's generation meets at Pine Hills High School where Emilia is a teacher with Alberto, Tina, and Darren. It is through their eyes and experiences that you will examine yourself and your classroom.

- Emilia is Italian American and is the granddaughter of Michael.
- Alberto is Mexican American and is the grandson of Teresa.
- Tina is white and her grandfather is James Robert, who migrated from Appalachia.
- Darren is African American and is the grandson of Charles.

This era of accountability has ushered in a new focus on teaching practices in service of students from low-income and impoverished communities. As with all students, effective teachers in low-income and impoverished communities are intentional in their relationship with students and in knowledge of their craft. Culturally proficient teachers meld relational and technical approaches in ways that value and build on the cultures students bring to school.

Emilia Takes Us Into the 21st Century

Though it is midway through the fall semester, Emilia finds that the STA professional development session is causing her to view students in her class in ways that she had not prior to the weekend retreat. She decided to follow one presenter's advice to focus her attention on three students as a means to reflect on her instructional practice. She selected Alberto, Tina, and Darren in order to give her a diverse set of students, each from an impoverished family.

Emilia gave her class an assignment to find a poem, rap, or narrative selection that they thought reflected or resonated with their personal stories. There was a lot of discussion about what resonated meant, but after a brief repartee the students seemed to understand that it reflected something that "fit" or was personally relevant. When something resonates between or among people, it means that they "get it" even if they have not shared the experience. After the resonance issue was settled, the students seemed to rally around the assignment and liked the fact that they had choice. Darren brought a poem written by a woman who had been in foster care most of her life. She was a speaker at a foster care retreat he attended. He really liked her and her message. Darren was the first to complete the assignment, and he was proud of his poem.

He asked if he could read it to her. With a strong voice, he read selected passages from Tanika's story:

Defending My Destiny[2]

I am more than a label!

You've grown accustomed to stereotyping me . . .

I make NO apologies for the LIFE

That was destiny for me!

I don't ask for your sympathy, merely a helping HAND

To assist me rather than underestimate me

In this battle for LIFE.

. . .

You've obtained your perception based on what society

Tells you I should be!

My story, IRRELEVANT

My pain, FORTHRIGHT

My experiences have forced many people to take flight.

My sabotage, my fears, my anger, my tears

Have ALL gone unrecognized!

Instead you label me and force this WHITE man's

THEORY to "better understand me!"

Yet, time and time again your ears have been closed

Sincerely unable to listen.

. . .

Resiliency is innate, it's already in me and although

I haven't lived the best of experiences they've each DEFINED

The essence of me.

So you may ask, why does her spoken word sound so angry and mad?!?

I'll shake my head because again, you'll try to analyze or personalize

My grief.

You'll attempt to "SAVE" me when this LIFE lesson is based on my

ABILITY to grow and be ENHANCED based on the discovery of

A reshaped me!

. . .

I've used EDUCATION to empower MYSELF

THUS, the reason for my existing and REFUSING to FAIL.

Being motivated by a drug called KNOWLEDGE

Has created a lens that even SOCIETY can't dismantle.

Society has to accept, acknowledge, OR co-exist.

To adequately understand the dimensions that persist in me,

You gotta (got to) be less quick to judge & open to listen

Because a LABEL does NOT define me . . . I've created a self-Made

Definition.

I determine my DESTINY!

Source: Written by Taniko King. © 2007 All copyrights belong exclusively to Taniko King.

Emilia wept as Darren read the poem. He read with prosody and clarity. Emilia wasn't aware that he even had that ability. And that made her cry. She cried again when she read Darren's reasons for selecting that particular poem. She realized Darren has a story, too, which provided even more impetus to continue with her commitment to studying her students so she could learn how to better structure her curricular and instructional choices.

In deciding which students to study, Emilia recalled from an early October parent conference with Tina's grandmother that they had recently been homeless again. Though she believed that her university preparation to teach in the Pine Hills School District was academically rigorous and aligned with emerging professional standards, she was beginning to see that it did not fully prepare her for how to mitigate the conditions of poverty that existed for students like Alberto, Tina, and Darren. Emilia has turned her attention to one of the handouts from the STA retreat, the Cultural Proficiency Curriculum and Instruction Rubric (see Table 4.2).

Table 4.2   Curriculum and Instruction Rubric

Five Essential Elements	Cultural Destructiveness	Cultural Incapacity	Cultural Blindness	Cultural Precompetence	Cultural Competence	Cultural Proficiency
Assessing Cultural Knowledge. Extent to which curriculum provides opportunities for educators and students to learn about self and others.	Limit or prohibit sharing of cultural knowledge and developing cultural identity.	Promote assimilation to the dominant culture and dominant learning styles and language.	Ignore aspects of culture (staff or students) that connects culture and learning.	Recognizing that the curriculum does not include students' cultural perspectives. Incorporate into the curriculum information and resources that may reflect students' perspectives.	Regularly provide opportunities for students to contribute their knowledge and perspectives about a lesson's topic(s) and use the knowledge to plan and sequence the lesson.	Assess the gap between the teacher's culture, the culture of the curriculum, and the culture of the students and seek ongoing opportunities to learn about and use culturally responsive curriculum.
Valuing Diversity. Extent to which curriculum reflects diversity.	Select and implement curriculum and use resources that denigrate specific perspectives, or groups, and/or provide incomplete or inaccurate portrayals of events, individuals, or groups.	Select and implement curriculum and use resources that reflect dominant group values, perspectives, and language.	Implement curriculum and use resources and languages recommended by state educational agencies and publishers, thereby providing limited cultural perspectives.	Recognize that curriculum may provide limited cultural perspectives. Select and develop supplemental curriculum and resources that provide information about contributions of diverse groups.	Select, develop, and implement curricula that reflect diverse perspectives and languages and provide inclusive, accurate portrayal of historical events and cultural groups.	Promote and develop students' advocacy for social justice.

Five Essential Elements	Cultural Destructiveness	Cultural Incapacity	Cultural Blindness	Cultural Precompetence	Cultural Competence	Cultural Proficiency
Managing the Dynamics of Difference. Extent to which curriculum promotes multiple perspectives.	Ignore, seek, or alter data to validate the placement of students into rigid, limiting curricular paths that provide negative educational consequences for all students.	View the core program as meeting the needs of all students. Underperforming students are tracked into rigid curricular paths judged to be the most effective approach to assimilate and advance students.	Implement only mandated state and federal curriculum and interventions determined to be of maximum benefit to underperforming students.	Recognizing that the curriculum may not be accessible to all students, teachers may differentiate instruction, at times inappropriately providing less challenging lessons for underperforming students.	Provide students curriculum options that are challenging and incorporate inquiry and higher-order thinking skills that personalize connections and evoke multiple perspectives. Underperforming students receive ongoing, timely, and personalized support from peers, teachers, and parents.	Provide students opportunities to learn how to learn—develop academic ability, intellective competence, and advocacy for social justice.
Adapting to Diversity. Extent to which cultural knowledge is integrated into the curriculum.	Select and use curriculum that perpetuates inaccurate and/or negative portrayal of diverse groups and historical events.	Use curriculum that portrays values and behaviors of the dominant group to promote the assimilation of diverse groups.	Embrace standards, standardized curriculum, resources, textbooks, and standardized tests to ensure	Recognizing students' cultural differences, curriculum may be supplemented with information about cultural contributions or	Integrate and infuse into existing curriculum culturally relevant content and differentiated instructional approaches/resources to meet the needs of all students.	Promote multiple perspectives in the curriculum to model and develop advocacy practices for social justice.

(Continued)

Table 4.2 (Continued)

Five Essential Elements	Cultural Destructiveness	Cultural Incapacity	Cultural Blindness	Cultural Precompetence	Cultural Competence	Cultural Proficiency
	Curriculum denigrates culturally different groups and events through omissions, distortions, and fallacious assumptions.	Staff believes that assimilation is integral to success.	equality across the curriculum for all student groups without regard for cultural differences.	events without integrating such into the curriculum.		
Institutionalizing. Extent to which values and policies support culturally responsive curriculum.	Create policies and practices that ensure a curriculum that excludes, denigrates, and misrepresents diverse groups and historical events. Actively pursue the identification and elimination of perspectives that threaten the desired perspective.	Create policies and practices that protect agency-sanctioned curriculum and instructional approaches while justifying them as beneficial for assimilating culturally different groups.	Standardize agency-sanctioned curriculum and instructional resources to meet the needs of all student groups.	Recognizing the limitation of the existing curriculum to be culturally responsive, staff may integrate culturally responsive approaches and materials.	Create policies and practices to ensure that agency-sanctioned curriculum is enhanced with information, instructional approaches, and resources to maximize the learning of all students. Strategies to ensure student success are articulated vertically and horizontally across grade levels and departments within schools and between feeder schools. Students, staff and parents regularly collaborate to examine data leading to continuous improvement of the curriculum program.	Enthusiastically embrace a districtwide responsibility for closing learning and achievement gaps.

Source: Adapted from *Culturally Proficient Inquiry: A Lens for Identifying and Examining Educational Gaps* (2008). Lindsey, Randall B., Graham, Stephanie, Westphal, Jr., R. Chris, & Jew, Cynthia. Thousand Oaks, CA: Corwin.

Emilia: [Ruminating over the Cultural Proficiency Curriculum and Instruction Rubric in the late afternoon quiet after all students have left for the day, she is oblivious to the fact that her colleague Jose has entered the room.]

Jose: That must be an intriguing article you are reading! Hey, let's call it a day and meet for a cup of coffee. I am not due to pick up my son from karate practice until 5 p.m. so I have an hour to kill and would like to catch up with you. It has been too long since we checked in with one another.

Emilia: Oh, hi, Jose. I was just lost in this article and thinking about the STA session I attended this weekend.

Jose: Hmm, what makes it so intriguing?

Emilia: Well, you and I share a passion for being able to succeed with PHHS students, particularly with impoverished kids like Alberto and Tina.

Jose: Yes, but how does that keep us from having coffee?

Emilia: Of course it doesn't! In fact, I will bring this with me so I can share it with you. It's so interesting. I think it is going to help me change how I am running my classroom and responding to my students. I went to the STA session this weekend to learn about how poverty impacts our kids, and I ended up learning a lot about myself. I realized I have to examine how I view the students every bit as much as my instructional program—they are linked together in ways that I had not realized!

Jose: What are you talking about?

Emilia: I learned that though I can't necessarily change the socioemotional or material conditions that our students face outside this school, I do control what happens in this classroom. Not only that, I have a moral responsibility to this community to educate every student.

Jose: [in a mocking voice] Sounds like you had a therapeutic weekend.

Emilia: Hey, that is not fair. You are as interested as I to see these kids succeed. No, what you may be seeing in me is the recognition that a generation ago my parents were in the same positions as Alberto, Tina, and Darren. I was once a "Tina." Homelessness could have been my fate had my

> grandmother not come to my parents' rescue. I never really thought of the incredible bullet that we dodged by living with my grandmother. She had food; we did not. She made sure our clothes were clean and presentable.

Jose: [He looks inquiringly at Emilia, as if to say, "Whoa, this is real!"]

Emilia: Jose, I am telling you all of this because I don't think we can teach students we don't know. I am beginning to think our relationships with the students are paramount to their achievement. I am through with the reminiscing— let's go for coffee; I want to share with you how I am going to study myself within my own classroom.

Emilia is beginning the next phase of her own education. She is going to focus on three students in her classroom as a means to improve instruction. The Cultural Proficiency Curriculum and Instruction Rubric will serve as a guide in a self-study of her instructional effectiveness.

Culturally Competent Praxis

Teachers who perceive themselves as effective are more likely to collaborate with peers, plan instruction, review data to check student output, and request input from peers (Jerald, 2007). Furthermore, when teachers have a strong belief that their individual performance is efficacious, and that their collective team is capable, a form of collective teacher efficacy (CTE) emerges. This emergence reflects a belief where teachers assess that they have a positive effect on student achievement (Goddard, Hoy, & Hoy, 2000). This belief seems to mitigate the effects of those circumstances that are usually thought to negatively impact student achievement.

Goddard, Hoy, and Hoy (2000) confirmed Albert Bandura's earlier work (1993) that CTE can reduce the negative effects of socioeconomic status and other class differences. When teachers believe in themselves and their colleagues, they are more likely to reach out to the community of parents and guardians (Ross & Gray, 2006), and they are more committed to the work that they do and the goals that they establish together.

Culturally proficient teaching encompasses a value for relationships and technical competency in one's craft. These two components, relationship building with students and technical competency, are foundational to culturally proficient pedagogy. When we as educators see ourselves in relationship to the community we serve, we are better prepared to have assumptions that are based in what's possible for our students. Understanding one's assumptions informs the cognitive, or technical, aspect of our teaching and the intentional choices made about instructional approaches and ways in which to select and present curriculum.

Technical Teaching

Teaching from a "technical" base, the teacher organizes her work from a cognitive standpoint, a thinking perspective. She is very diligent about moving students from the place of getting information to being able to use information; most of all, she wants to see results. Technical teachers know their curriculum and the written requirements of their responsibilities.

Relational Teaching

Teaching from a "relational" base, the teacher organizes his work from a humanistic perspective. He develops relationships with students as a starting place to teach course content. He operates from his ability to create a *trust-generating* climate where students construct meaning from their individual point of view in balance with their prior experience. Paulo Freire (1995), educational philosopher and literacy expert, believed this relationship between teacher and student to be important:

> The educator's efforts must be imbued with a profound trust in people and their creative power. To achieve this, the humanist educator must be a partner of the students in [. . .] relations with them. From this perspective, the teacher shares the classroom and the responsibility for learning with the students. Trust becomes a foundation for a caring learning experience that often attracts students to continued pursuit of knowledge. (p. 72)

Relational teachers use their genuine openness to support the trust process and allow students to know how they feel about the issues that are related to what is being taught.

Table 4.3 presents key ideas related to technical and relational teaching aligned with the three points on the right side, the positive side, of the Cultural Proficiency Continuum—cultural precompetence, cultural competence, and cultural proficiency. Please note the Continuum is developmental and cumulative, meaning that behaviors and attitudes listed in cultural precompetence are carried forward into cultural competence.

Table 4.3   The Cultural Proficiency Continuum Aligned With Technical and Relational Teaching

Transformation for Equity		
Cultural Precompetence	**Cultural Competence**	**Cultural Proficiency**
Technical Teaching	**Relational Teaching**	**Relational Teaching**
• Relies on cognitive approaches to teaching—the thinking curriculum • Focuses on academic outcomes of course or grade level • Provides observable structure for students • Functions well with students who are motivated to learn • Relies on technical knowledge of others' cultures • Knows traditions, artifacts, and rituals of cultures • Begins to "know what they don't know about student cultures"	• Possesses skills of technical teaching • Is sensitive, often at an intuitive level, to the nuances of cultural norms, beliefs, laws, mores, customs, and habits • Approaches education from an inclusive humanistic, or relational, worldview • Values building relationships with students as a foundational building block of teaching • Fosters a climate of trust building • Views self as a partner with students in their co-learning • Demonstrates trust in self and students. • Students believe the teacher is invested in their success	• Possesses skills of technical and relational teaching • Commits to own life-long learning • Demonstrates commitment to education as a social justice issue • Demonstrates advocacy for students

Culturally Proficient Teaching

The preferred instructional practice for the poverty classroom combines "relational" and "technical" approaches. Culturally proficient teaching responds to very specific needs in the typical classroom serving the grandchildren and great-grandchildren of Michael, Charles, James Robert, and Teresa. The new paradigm provides

- A relational focus in a student-centered process (Greenwood, 1997; Greenwood, Delquadri, & Carta 1988),
- A culture of success fostered for all students (Delpit, 1995),
- Explicit learning objectives to manage data and information (Love, 2009; Skrla, McKenzie, & Scheurich, 2009),

- Content standards as a base (Kendall & Marzano, 2004),
- Educators committed to pedagogy that builds on the culture the students bring to school (Banks, 1999; Hollins, 2008), and
- Where students develop the moral aptitude to consider individual, community, and global impact for values, beliefs, and decisions to combat bullying, classist and racist acts, depression, chronic health problems, anxiety, and abuse (Hollins, 2008; Jones, 2009).

The Cultural Proficiency paradigm has as its priority the development of a moral, democratic society with equal educational outcomes for all students (Terrell & Lindsey, 2009). We can no longer tolerate getting by with focusing on our *willingness* to provide equal opportunities. We need to provide equitable opportunities through the manner in which we conduct our classrooms and organize our schools. To provide guidance, Nuri-Robins, Lindsey, Lindsey, & Terrell (2006) describe culturally proficient instruction as

- A mind-set that guides instructors and builds confidence and competence.
- The use of specific tools for effectively describing, responding to, and planning for issues and opportunities that emerge in diverse environments.
- A way of becoming and growing as an educator.

Using the essential elements of cultural competence, culturally proficient educators have the skill and will to demonstrate these behaviors:

- Valuing the learner as thinker and doer,
- Honoring and respecting the cultural identities of all learners,
- Designing experiences that build on prior knowledge and experiences of the learner,
- Understanding assessment bias,
- Holding high expectations for each learner,
- Presenting rigorous, standards-based content,
- Selecting materials and resources that reflect multicultural perspectives,
- Managing the dynamics of difference, and
- Valuing diversity and inclusion (pp. 31–32).

10 Tenets for Asset-Based Learning

Culturally proficient educators work with students from low-income and impoverished communities from an asset-based perspective with known effective instructional strategies and approaches. We have adapted Haberman's work and combined it with our experiences to create 10 Tenets to Build Asset-Based Learning Communities. Each tenet contributes to the development of relational teaching in a classroom and school where learning can occur and negative forces in students' lives can be mitigated. In displaying these tenets, it is to be understood that learning communities exist at two levels: the students in our classrooms and among the educators at our schools.

These statements are to guide teachers' own personal work and their work with colleagues to inform the skills and desire they want to model with and for their students.

- *Accept and respect difference.* Inclusion is a norm in all aspects of the learning community of students and the educators. Ensure that educators and students experience themselves as facilitators of acceptance and inclusion. Provide students a safe harbor for handling disrespect and hate in the classroom, school, and outside community.
- *Acknowledge choices in life.* Help all members of the learning community understand that their choices matter, not their circumstances. Be certain to set boundaries for negotiables and non-negotiables. For example, it may be negotiated to have an assignment be late but racial or sexually explicit language is not permitted.
- *Stop distractions.* Ensure that the climate is right to stay focused on the work of school. School leaders need to mitigate disruptions into the school day, and teachers must maintain classrooms that provide the opportunity for students to work with few interruptions. We must teach students to be responsible for focusing on the academic tasks before us and to turn off personal chatter that, though important to them, must wait until a different time.
- *Teach and use personal reflection.* Educators and students view success as theirs to measure, claim, and honor when they focus on doing the right things for the greater good. Reflection is a skill that will never go to the depth necessary for change in self without the will to guide it. For educators and our students, it is our experience that reflection must be intentionally taught. Use questions like those posed throughout this book to guide the development of reflective questions for you and for your students.
- *Care and invest in others.* Educators and students step outside themselves to be in service to others. In other words, move from "me" to "we." Ask questions that prompt interest about and concern for others. This is an important lesson for being a citizen in our democracy.

- *Act responsibly and consider others.* Discover the assets, talents, and capital that can become commodities for one's own success but also examine errors, miscues, and mistakes to ensure a lifetime of growth not stagnation. Strive to harm no one. Make amends without being prompted when harm does occur. Keep your slate as clean as possible.
- *Believe and behave knowing that humans are self-righting.* Use positive actions and language to describe students, their families, and their potential. Let your colleagues and your students see, hear, and experience your belief in their ability to become successful, to improve, or to redirect their energy to more positive and prosocial outcomes.
- *Identify what is important, non-negotiable, a must-have to facilitate learning.* Utilize whatever tools necessary to teach information, knowledge, concepts, and theories acknowledging that no long-term learning happens without linking emotion and meaning.
- *Collaborate and be responsive.* Organize, plan, and deliver for students by having an interactive, visual classroom that reflects who the students are and where they have been. Model collaboration, cooperation, and community as components of an effective learning community.
- *Commit to do what is right.* Help students value their contributions to the common good and their service to making an improvement in the social conditions of people in the classroom, school, and community. Use instructional devices such as the Socratic method to explore and develop understanding of underlying ethical and value issues.

Relational teaching, the 10 tenets for asset-based learning, and the right side of the rubric are inextricably interlinked. Relational teaching is based on a sound base of technical competence. The 10 tenets foster asset development for educators and students alike. The Essential Elements of Cultural Competence serve as the standards for educator values and behaviors and for schools' policies and practices. In the next vignette, Emilia shares her insights when using the rubric as a means of assessing herself.

Emilia and the Rubric

Emilia is fully aware of the pressures that have emerged on schools to improve their performance with students from all low socioeconomic groups within our communities. The complexity of schools in terms of issues of poverty, English learners, assessment/accountability, learning communities, homeless youth, and foster youth are not lost on her.

However, she also understands that just a few years ago there was great resistance to desegregation of schools along the lines of race, ofdenying/limiting access to female students in mathematics and science, and in marginalizing special-needs students.

Of the many things that still resonate with Emilia from the STA retreat were the many manifestations of resistance to change that exist within schools. Personally, she recognized that she had become comfortable with the status quo in her own regard for students and that she had become quiescent when hearing colleagues talk about "these students" or the "project kids" or the "trailer park kids." However, she also knew that her advocacy had to begin with her own performance in her own classroom. So, she sat with the Cultural Proficiency Curriculum and Instruction Rubric and began to plot where she saw her instruction with regard to Alberto, Tina, and Darren. Once she completed that assessment, she planned to do as the STA presenters had suggested and make the assessment for how she envisioned her department and the school responding to the educational needs of students like Alberto, Tina, and Darren.

Jose: Hi, Emilia! I got your e-mail regarding your rubric self-assessment. What's up? How can I help?

Emilia: Well, it is not a pretty picture.

Jose: Meaning?

Emilia: Well, the STA presenters implored us to approach using the rubric and to be honest in our assessment and not to make the assessment for how we would "like to be."

Jose: So, no halo effect, eh?

Emilia: Exactly! Particularly when I look at the "10 Tenets," too! They clearly align with the right side of the continuum.

Jose: What did you find?

Emilia: Do you recall the Five Essential Elements on the rubric?

Jose: I recall you mentioned they were standards and at the use of that term, I rolled my eyes.

Emilia: True, but when we read them together they made sense to both of us. Also, remember that you offered to coach me in this process?

Jose: Sure, you are right.

Emilia: Well, my highest self-rating was "Valuing Diversity," where I rated myself at "Precompetence," and for all the others I was at "Cultural Blindness."

Jose: Wow! Oh, I am sorry, that is not a very good coaching response. But, couldn't you be running the risk of being a bit harsh on yourself?

Emilia: No, not at all. If I am not going to be honest with myself, how else can I improve? My only other alternative is to say it's the kids' fault and throw my hands up in despair!

Jose: And, neither of us is about to do that. There is enough of that at PHHS already. So, let me start again. Focusing on any one of the essential elements, what can you do differently that may improve your instructional approach with your three students?

Emilia: Well, it is interesting. As I continued to study the rubric last night, it became clear to me that even though my family came from communities like these kids, I know very little about their cultural backgrounds—from either an ethnic or social-class experience. The second learning is that even though I am one of the loudest voices in support of standards-based approaches to instruction and assessment, I have not paid enough attention to differentiated approaches to my instruction.

Jose: And, what does this mean for you?

Emilia: These are things I can learn. I have the will to see what these kids can do instead of focusing on what they can't do. It is as much my approach to working with them as it is their response to me and to the school. I guess by the time many kids get to high school they have learned to be non-achievers.

Reflection

Think about Emilia for a moment. Think about her reflective-ness. Are you prepared to do the same for your role within your classroom or school? What is it within you that supports being reflective about your pedagogy? What are the forces that may struggle against your being reflective? Use the space below to record your response.

_____

_____

_____

_____

_____

In Chapter 5, we continue with Emilia in her role as a non-formal leader at Pine Hills High School. Emilia moves from the personal use of reflection, a discussion with self, to dialogue with colleagues, a discussion with others.

Going Deeper

In what ways do you describe Emilia as a non-formal leader? How do you describe her as a learner? What are you learning?

_____

_____

_____

_____

_____

_____

Notes

1. The term *praxis* refers to the practical skill of teaching and pedagogy to the profession of teaching.
2. Taniko's story, a real person's story, appears in its entirety in Resource C.

5

Culturally Proficient Leadership Support for Instruction

Invite in everybody who cares to work on what's possible.
Acknowledge that everyone is an expert about something. Know
that creative solutions come from new connections.

—Margaret Wheatley, 2002, p. 145

Getting Centered

"Poverty and Social Justice," thought Emilia. That's the theme that she wants to bring to the Pine Hills' Leadership Team! Since the school cautiously embraced the concept of Learning Communities three years ago, they had begun to work on curricular standards, accountability issues related to state testing, parent-community relationships, and instructional improvement. The weekend retreat with the State Teachers' Association (STA) had sparked a light in her that took her back to fond remembrances of her childhood, her immigrant grandparents, and recalling the limited resources they had. More important, she was seeing more clearly that many educators in her school were just going through the motions of knowing the students from the Pine Hills community.

How would educators at your school respond to being involved with an examination of poverty and social justice at your school? Use the space below to record your response and to comment on Emilia's imminent proposal.

_____

_____

_____

_____

Emilia approached the principal and the faculty chairperson of the School Leadership Team (SLT) and proposed Poverty and Social Justice as a theme for addressing the chronic underachievement of students from low-income homes and conditions of poverty and as a way to introduce academic optimism into conversations.

Principal: Emilia, I am very interested to hear what you learned during your retreat and how it may inform our work at Pine Hills.

SLT Teacher: I am, too, Emilia. You and I have had many conversations over the years about ways in which we can motivate these kids to learn. So, what did you learn?

Emilia: Well, this may come as a major surprise but I didn't learn as much about students from poverty as I learned how little I know about our students or how our students may experience this school.

Principal: I don't follow.

SLT Teacher: Emilia, don't tell me this was another of those programs where the school and the educators are the bad guys and "we just don't get it!"

Emilia: No, not that at all. We discussed, in depth, the social inequities that cause poverty to persist in our country. However, we also discussed that poverty is too often used as an excuse for not challenging ourselves, and our students, to perform at ever-higher levels.

SLT Teacher: Hmmm. I must admit that I am skeptical, but I can see you are intent. So, what did you learn?

Emilia: Well, for openers, we used the tools of cultural proficiency to focus on issues of poverty and devised a set of beliefs that I would like to pose to our School

Leadership Team that might guide our learning communities this year. Here, take a look at this copy of the belief statements:

- Formal and non-formal leaders view the school as an agency that provides the benefits of a democratic society to all students.
- Leaders focus on educators exploring and understanding the basis for their assumptions about poverty, as well as the conditions of poverty.
- Leaders focus on knowing, in authentic ways, the community the school serves.
- Leaders hold teaching as the most important adult activity at the school.
- Leaders promote a sense of curiosity about the interrelationship of the curriculum, the instruction, student learning, and social justice.

SLT Teacher: You did have quite a retreat! To be honest, Emilia, I am uncomfortable with these beliefs focusing on administrators only. If this is going to be successful, teachers can't be invisible. We must be involved, too!

Principal: You know, that was my initial reaction, too, but if we stop and think for a minute Pine Hills High School is trying to diffuse leadership in a way that involves more of us in decision making.

Emilia: Precisely! And, not just how the budget is carved up among the various departments and functions but, more important, how we hold the education of our students as the sole purpose for having this school.

Principal: As we're talking I am thinking about the administrator certification program that I teach in at Central Local University (CLU). We have been studying the emerging standards for leadership development, and they are not a lot different from what you have here.

Emilia, the SLT teacher, and the principal begin planning how to engage members of the Pine Hills faculty to view Poverty and Social Justice as a lens for their work. They realize this is a bold move, fraught with all kinds of problems, but they realize that it is the moral thing to do. The Learning Community is an appropriate vehicle for leading this inquiry and the dialogue that accompanies the inquiry.

The vignettes in this chapter illustrate the planning that Emilia, the SLT teacher, and principal do to begin the inquiry to guide themselves and their colleagues in exploring assumptions that are embedded in educator behaviors and school practices. As their first task, they have assembled five tables to array the statements about poverty aligned with professional standards for school leadership and the essential elements of cultural competence. Tables 5.1 to 5.5 are the centerpieces for this chapter.

Intent of This Chapter

This chapter relates the manner in which adaptive leaders intentionally use the talents of all members of the school community to achieve equitable educational opportunity for all students. As you read this chapter, note that we have intertwined three important components to illustrate their interdependence:

- The emergent professional standards for school leadership.
- The belief statements introduced by Emilia.
- The Essential Elements of Cultural Competence introduced in Chapter 3.

The interdependence of the leadership standards, beliefs about poverty, and the essential elements of cultural competence demonstrates the importance of making the education of all socioeconomic classes of students the core work of our schools. Our role as educators is to express academic optimism in support of people from low-income and impoverished communities having access to the social, economic, and political arenas in democratic societies.

Leadership for Learning

Standards for school leaders have emerged in recent years to guide the work of school administrators, and we are presenting them as central to the work of non-formal school leaders as well. Standards for schools, teachers, and administrators embed professional responsibility for equity, social justice, and closing the achievement gap in learning (National Policy Board for Educational Administration [NPBEA], 2008). Modern leadership standards for school leaders in the United States began with the Interstate School Leaders Licensure Consortium (1996) and was updated by the NPBEA. The leadership standards describe six areas of leadership that have been adopted, or adapted, in 40 states.

We have adapted the NPBEA leadership standards to focus on providing formal and non-formal school leaders the tools to provide each and every student with the education necessary to enjoy full participation in a democratic society. Each of the NPBEA's six standards of leadership helps frame what leaders, both formal and non-formal, need to do to realize the mission and vision of schools and infuse academic optimism as operational within their practice as school leaders. The six standards for education leaders (Sanders & Kearney, 2008) are the following:

1. Vision, Mission, and Goals

Education leaders ensure the achievement of all students by guiding the development and implementation of a shared vision of learning, strong organizational mission, and high expectations for every student.

2. Teaching and Learning

Education leaders ensure achievement and success of all students by monitoring and continuously improving teaching and learning.

3. Managing Organizational Systems and Safety

Education leaders ensure the success of all students by managing organizational systems and resources for a safe, high-performing learning environment.

4. Collaborating With Families and Stakeholders

Education leaders ensure the success of all students by collaborating with families and stakeholders who represent diverse community interests and needs and mobilizing community resources that improve teaching and learning.

5. Ethics and Integrity

Education leaders ensure the success of all students by being ethical and acting with integrity.

6. The Education System

Education leaders ensure the success of all students by influencing interrelated systems of political, social, economic, legal, and cultural contexts affecting education to advocate for their teachers' and students' needs.

As you can see, there is nothing in the standards that precludes addressing the education of students from low-income and impoverished communities. However, transition from standards to beliefs to actions is the work of school leaders. Emilia developed a set of belief statements for educators working in low-income and impoverished communities designed to guide the professional educational leader standards and the Essential Elements of Cultural Competence.

Tables 5.1 through 5.5 each present one or more professional standards, aligned with a belief statement about poverty and one or more essential elements of cultural competence. As you read each of the Tables 5.1 to 5.5, please note that the professional standards for school leaders appear in the first column, the belief statements about poverty in the second column, and the essential elements of cultural competence are in the third column. This chapter is organized using the beliefs about poverty statements to describe and discuss the role of formal and non-formal school leaders. The roles of school leaders are presented as conforming to professional standards established by the National Policy Board for Educational Administration (2008). The essential elements of cultural competence are the complementary standards that reinforce the belief statements about poverty and the professional standards for educational leaders.

Reflective and Dialogic Questions

Chapters 1 through 4 provided reflective questions to guide your thinking, to probe your values, and to consider new ways to respond to students from low-income and impoverished communities. In this chapter we introduce dialogic questions. Dialogic questions are intended for you and your colleagues to think together, to probe individual and school values, and to explore new ways of responding to and interacting with students from low-income and impoverished communities.

Belief 1: Formal and Non-Formal Leaders View the School as an Agency That Provides the Benefits of a Democratic Society to All Students

Please refer to Table 5.1 that illustrates the alignment of

- Two standards for professional leaders—advocacy and managing systems—and
- The essential element—valuing diversity—with
- The belief statement about poverty—schools as an agency that provides benefits of democracy to all students.

Table 5.1   Alignment of Professional Standards of Advocacy and Managing
Systems With Belief Statements About Poverty and Essential Elements

Professional Standards for Educational Leaders	Belief Statements for Schools Serving Communities of Poverty	Essential Elements of Cultural Competence
Education leaders ensure the success of all students by influencing interrelated systems of political, social, economic, legal, and cultural contexts affecting education to advocate for their teachers' and students' needs.	Formal and non-formal leaders view the school as an agency that provides the benefits of a democratic society to all students.	Value Diversity
Education leaders ensure the success of all students by managing organizational systems and resources for a safe, high-performing learning environment.		Manage the Dynamics of Difference

Note the consistency of the action verbs among the three columns—ensuring, advocating, and valuing.

The core purpose and mission of Canadian and U.S. schools over the last century has been to serve as a vehicle to becoming a full-fledged Canadian or American, in other words an active member in a democratic society. Documents from the first third of the 20th century refer to citizenship socialization as a function of schooling. School records that tracked students born in Canada or the United States recorded their immigrant status and the birthplace of their parents. In the United States, African American boys' and girls' progress toward becoming literate and becoming useful citizens was tracked (Keyssar, 2002).

Finally, after 30 years of muted response, policymakers and school-level school leaders have begun to react to analyses of disaggregated data which reveals differential achievement levels by race, gender, language acquisition, and special needs. At the national, provincial, and state levels of Canada and the United States, policies have been created that mandate data collection, provide additional resources for needy schools, and provide firm accountability measures (NCLB, 2002; Ontario Ministry of Education, 2009; Perie, Moran, & Lutkus, 2005). States, provinces, and large districts intervene with a prescriptive reliance on adopted instructional materials designed to unify classroom practice, and in some cases accelerate learning for students who are not academically successful. Some schools took the challenge to heart and began to examine their own practices, attitudes, and expectations. As an example, one school that we visited began to establish policies that were not negotiable, such as "All students can and will learn, parents must be involved in the education of our students. They're all of our kids." Literacy and achieving grade level standards became expected norms. If the child failed, we failed and we must find what it takes to be successful in teaching each and every child. These educators believed in their mission statements and were working to realize Americanization and participating in a democracy as their personal mission and vision.

The Pine Hills' Learning Community

In the first vignette, the planning committee of the PHLC has begun to study the tables provided by Emilia as an advance organizer to better understand the professional standards for school leaders, the belief statements about poverty, and the essential elements of cultural competence. Let's see what they have to say about Table 5.1.

Emilia:	Well, putting these tables together certainly has shown how these three sources overlap and interrelate!
SLT Teacher:	Yes, is certainly has. Now we have to figure out what to do with it.
Principal:	Well, for openers, I am pleased that our faculty is informed about cultural proficiency. That will be most helpful.
Emilia:	I am beginning to see what a gargantuan task this is. Are you telling me that in your administrator-preparation program at CLU that you actually get into all of this social, economic, political, and cultural contexts stuff?
Principal:	Yes, just the way we did in our teacher preparation program. I am embarrassed to say, I didn't pay enough attention then.
SLT Teacher:	Well, what I take from this is the role of advocacy. It is easy to say, but challenging to do. I have a friend who teaches in a large school district, and he is proud to be a member of a social justice committee in his teachers' union. I'll check with him to get some ideas for what they are doing.
Emilia:	Hmm. I think that is a good idea, but I do have a question for him. Given the history of the labor movement in North America as an advocate, why isn't the entire union an advocate for our students? Why is it the function of a committee?

Principal: The same could be asked of our administrators' organizations and unions and our boards of education!

Dialogue Questions for You and Your Colleagues

What are the avenues—in your school, district, community,
province, or state—in which you should be involved as an advocate
for students from low-income and impoverished communities? What
would advocacy look like for you in these contexts? What would
advocacy look like in your daily contact with your students, their
parents or guardians, community members, and your colleagues?
Please use the space below to record your personal thoughts and the
insights you gain from dialogue with colleagues.

_____

_____

_____

_____

Belief 2: Leaders Focus on Educators Exploring and Understanding the Basis for Their Assumptions About Poverty, as Well as the Conditions of Poverty

Table 5.2 provides for the following alignment:

- The standard for professional leaders—ethics,
- The essential elements—assessing cultural knowledge and managing the dynamics of difference—and
- The belief statement about poverty—assumptions about and conditions of poverty.

Table 5.2   Alignment of Professional Standards of Ethics With Belief Statements About Poverty and Essential Elements

Professional Standards for Educational Leaders	Belief Statements for Schools Serving Communities of Poverty	Essential Elements of Cultural Competence
Education leaders ensure the success of all students by being ethical and acting with integrity.	Leaders focus on educators exploring and understanding the basis for their assumptions about poverty, as well as the conditions of poverty.	Assess Cultural Knowledge and Manage the Dynamics of Difference

Note the action verb "ensuring" in the first column denotes professional standard is aligned with verbs that promote reflection and
dialogue in columns two and three—"exploring, understanding, assessing, and managing."

In recent memory, our schools have had a "disposable" lowest quartile of children, and "disposable" schools that serve to perpetuate the disenfranchisement of students who are from low-income and impoverished communities. Michael, James Robert, Teresa, and Charles, who we met in Chapter 2, had very different experiences and their children and grandchildren had different lives because their school systems provided separate and unequal opportunities for education. Teresa and Charles were subjected to "separate but equal" experiences while James Robert's educational experience was similarly limited due to economic conditions. Michael's family was able to take advantage of schooling opportunities and each generation was able to exert greater control over its economic, social, and political lives.

There are many factors in the culture of schools and schooling that have contributed to the attitude that some students are beyond help. The prevailing function of schools has been sorting and selecting some students as worthy of continuing on to college while others were channeled to options limited to work in low-skill and low-wages enterprises (Lemann, 1999). The lack of equitable, high standards for students from low-income and impoverished conditions were reflected in educators who acted as if students from low socioeconomic environs had deficits too great to overcome in school. Conditions such as these too often led to a seemingly disenfranchised citizenry with limited ability to read a newspaper analytically, to sponsor or choose candidates based on how prevailing issues affect them, and, in the case of Charles, Teresa, and their families, to determine where they could and could not reside.

Michael's granddaughter Emilia, now a teacher at Pine Hills High School, benefited from the legislation, policies, regulations, and local practices designed to improve student achievement. It may be that one of her best tools for helping students from low-income and impoverished conditions is her family's story, which is rooted in many of the same issues that her students are dealing with. For teachers who do not share a family story about being from low-income or impoverished communities, an important question may be, "How can we help to develop the awareness and the understanding of how to best serve the needs all children?"

The ethical connection among leadership, cultural proficiency, and working in low-income or impoverished communities may be informed by the instructive and concrete to-do list Paul Gorski provides in *The Myth of the Culture of Poverty* (Gorski, 2008).

- Educate ourselves about class and poverty.
- Reject deficit theory and help students and colleagues unlearn misperceptions about poverty.
- Make school involvement accessible to all families.

- Continue reaching out to low-income families even when they appear unresponsive (and without assuming, if they are unresponsive, that we know why).
- Respond when colleagues stereotype poor students or parents.
- Never assume that all students have equitable access to such learning resources as computers and the Internet, and never assign work requiring this access without providing in-school time to complete it.
- Ensure that learning materials do not stereotype poor people.
- Fight to keep low-income students from being assigned unjustly to special education or low academic tracks.
- Make curriculum relevant to poor students, drawing on and validating their experiences and intelligences.
- Teach about the antipoverty work of Martin Luther King Jr., Helen Keller, the Black Panthers, César Chávez, and other U.S. icons—and about why this dimension of their legacies has been erased from our national consciousness.
- Fight to ensure that school meal programs offer healthy options (p. 32).

Gorski (2008) follows by asking that we continue to do the inside-out work of examining our own assumptions and beliefs as they affect how we do the work of leading and that we examine and share data about our students. More important, he asks that we continue to examine our system that has failed so many students to date.

Table 5.2 poses some opportunities and risks for educators engaging in dialogue. It is an opportunity for knowing if you, your colleagues, and your school have engaged in the depth of reflection that reveals assumptions. This may be the pivot point of the inside-out change process in that it indicates the levels of willingness of moving beyond blaming others to responding to the question, "What am I willing to do to rectify the situation of disparate and chronic underachievement?"

The Pine Hills' Learning Community

SLT Teacher: Well, to quote my father, the information in this table will separate the men from the boys!

Principal: Most likely there is a more inclusive way of saying what you just said, but I do understand. In fact, I will be real honest with you. I don't want to engage in one of those blame-game activities where people are focused on being male, white, or middle class.

Emilia:	Hey, let's be honest. This is going to make some people feel uncomfortable mostly because we have not had to look at the data before. There may be levels of discomfort, but we have the responsibility to support our colleagues in our collective learning. This is about finding solutions and the resolve to provide for our students.
Principal:	While I agree with you, I am the one who received the negative feedback from disgruntled faculty and staff members.
SLT Teacher:	Then, we have the responsibility to ensure that this process is a community inquiry.
Emilia:	Truly! One of the things emphasized at the STA retreat is that when we begin this inquiry that it is a three- to five-year process.
Principal:	Three to five years! You must be kidding me.
Emilia:	Well, we didn't create these disparities in a few years, so it will take time to "right the ship!" But, and there is an important but . . .
SLT Teacher:	I sense a huge "however" coming.
Emilia:	We can't wait for three to five years to begin; we have to begin now and to measure our progress and setbacks. And the second however—we cannot waver in our commitments to ourselves and to these kids.

Dialogic Questions for You and Your Colleagues

In what ways are you willing to examine your assumptions about people from low-income and impoverished communities? In what ways are you willing to engage and support colleagues to examine their assumptions about people from low-income and impoverished communities? To what extent do the policies and practices in your school reflect healthy attitudes and assumptions? To what extent are assumptions about students embedded in policies and practices? Please use the space below to record your personal thoughts and the insights you gain from dialogue with colleagues.

_____

_____

_____

_____

Belief 3: Leaders Focus on Knowing, in Authentic Ways, the Community the School Serves

Table 5.3 illustrates the alignment of

- The standard for professional leaders—collaboration,
- The essential elements—adapting to diversity and institutionalizing cultural knowledge—with
- The belief statement about poverty—authentically knowing the community.

Table 5.3   Alignment of Professional Standards of Collaboration With Belief Statements About Poverty and Essential Elements

Professional Standards for Educational Leaders	Belief Statements for Schools Serving Communities of Poverty	Essential Elements of Cultural Competence
Education leaders ensure the success of all students by collaborating with families and stakeholders who represent diverse community interests and needs and mobilizing community resources that improve teaching and learning.	Leaders focus on knowing, in authentic ways, the community the school serves.	Adapt to Diversity and Institutionalize Cultural Knowledge

Note the consistency of the action verbs among the three columns—each deals with an aspect of learning. In this case, the learning is *our* learning. As with the other belief statements, it is about our becoming learning communities in which we commit to learning about the community we serve to be of best service to the children and youth who come to our schools.

Culturally proficient leaders continuously study the community they serve to discern needs and in what ways they can respond to needs. This leadership standard focuses on leaders' ability to collaborate with families and the community. Unless you are one of the very few who works and lives in the same community this is going to require some diligent work and relationship building. This type of relationship building often results into exploring "nested communities" (Berliner, 2009). The classroom resides in the school, the school within a district, and the school and district within diverse communities. Effective leadership engages each aspect of the school community to impact student learning.

Culturally proficient leaders continuously want to know what they don't know. They seek out information about their constituencies. They demonstrate respect for diverse opinions and cultures by reaching out to the constituent groups in the community who come in contact with their students. They employ multiple systems of communication with a variety of stakeholders to provide them with information about what's going on in the many communities represented in their school. These systems also provide feedback so that leaders know what the communities think and believe about the school and its leaders.

Culturally proficient educational leaders go into the community as a matter of routine practice. They issue invitations, and more important, they recognize the need to follow up so the invitation is viewed as authentic and will lead to meaningful engagement. They become members of community organizations, city commissions, religious organizations, and informal groups that can assist with educating children. They provide multiple ways to know about the school and its vision. Communications are translated, mailed, e-mailed, Twittered, and carried home in the backpacks of students. There is an effective use of all media to carry the messages of the school. There are representatives who are active and join community service clubs and organizations so that the school doesn't just show up when they need a scholarship once a year.

The school is seen as a hub of the community, bringing together the many neighborhoods and cultures represented in the school. As educational leaders move throughout the community, they become aware of the web of relationships and political influences within the community. Experienced leaders use this information to inform and develop policies that support learning and teaching in schools. They ask themselves, "Do I understand the larger political context of the school and community? Can I track the patterns of relationships and communications of community members represented in our school? How can I influence the policies that will affect our school? How do we bring the assets of each group into the decision making processes that affect learning and teaching?"

Education leaders are constantly advocating for what each group of students needs to do to be their best. While they uphold policies of each layer of governance above them, they also work to inform and change policies that are exclusionary or don't meet the needs of groups of students. Gathering and sharing data about every group of students can affect policy in important ways.

Table 5.3 takes us off campus and into the community. Collaboration with parents and community members signals a willingness and ability to know the community and to use that knowledge in ways that authenticate your students. When true collaboration occurs, the school is not located "within" the community, it "is" the community. Parents, guardians, and community members are not visitors—they are partners in the education of the children and youth from the community.

The Pine Hills' Learning Community

Emilia: Wow, this is going to be interesting!

SLT Teacher: In what way?

Principal: Emilia was born and raised in this community and is a PHHS graduate.

SLT Teacher: I think I knew that. Your passion for these kids has always been evident to most of us.

Emilia: Thanks, that feels good, but today I am like most everyone else at this school. I live 30 minutes from here. I drive to school using the same streets every day, I park in the locked parking space, and I make sure I am on my way home before the sun sets (which is quite early in the winter!) Being here for afterschool activities is always a chore!

Principal: Yes, that does define most of us. It sure does me! I couldn't uproot my family when this job came open. My kids are in good schools, and I promised them they could graduate from that high school.

SLT Teacher: And, we want the same for PHHS students, too!

Emilia: So, what Table 5.3 is telling me is there must be ways to get engaged with the community.

SLT Teacher: I have a cousin who teaches at an elementary school in Sacramento. The demographics are very similar to the Pine Hills' community. Their teachers initiated with their principal and teacher aides to actually organize meetings in the community, sometimes in homes, as a way to become familiar with the students' surroundings.

Dialogic Questions for You and Your Colleagues

How well do you know the community that your students live in when they are not at school? In what ways could you become familiar with the various features of the community your school serves? In what ways could you work together to mobilize resources in support of your students? Please use the space below to record your personal thoughts and the insights you gain from dialogue with colleagues.

_____

_____

_____

_____

Belief 4: Leadership Holds Teaching as the Most Important Adult Activity at the School

Table 5.4 shows the alignment of

- The standards for professional leaders—improving teaching and learning,
- The essential elements of valuing diversity and institutionalizing cultural knowledge, with
- The belief statement about poverty—teaching is the most important adult activity at the school.

Table 5.4   Alignment of Professional Standards of Improving Teaching With Belief Statements About Poverty and Essential Elements

Professional Standards for Educational Leaders	Belief Statements for Schools Serving Communities of Poverty	Essential Elements of Cultural Competence
Education leaders ensure achievement and success of all students by monitoring and continuously improving teaching and learning.	Leaders hold teaching as the most important adult activity at the school.	Value Diversity and Institutionalize Cultural Knowledge

Note the consistency among the columns—leadership in schools is all about teaching and learning. It is no more complicated than that. As educators working with students and parents or guardians from low-income and impoverished communities, we delve into our commitment of ensuring education, our assumptions about communities different from us, and our ability to collaborate in communities of poverty. In many schools, these are learning opportunities for educators to become practiced in differentiating instruction that meets the needs of diverse populations. For formal and non-formal school leaders this is an opportunity to commit to making teaching the central adult activity for the school.

Student achievement is tied to the ability of teachers to teach. Only if leaders focus on working with teachers to improve academic outcomes will there be any improvement in learning. The leadership standards provide two areas for guidance focused on developing a shared vision focused on learning and teaching.

Education leaders understand that the groups they lead have a variety of perspectives as related to being inclusive and are ready with strategies for dealing with the inevitable conflicts that will arise.

Beginning with an inventory of assumptions the educational leader must ask, "Do I believe that diversity in an organization is an asset or a hindrance to teaching and learning? Do I believe that adults should also be life-long learners? Do I value collaboration with everyone involved in our students' lives?"

Effective education leaders will begin to affect the culture of learning and teaching by gathering, processing, and sharing data in effective ways that build collaboration and an ever deeper understanding of learning and teaching. They will gather data about outcomes, demographics, and processes that have led to the current student results. They will acknowledge that there are multiple ways to meet the needs of a variety of learners and they will share effective practices among teachers and other stakeholders. Reducing isolation, basing discussion items and actions on observable data, finding ways for all students to reach grade-level competencies are the focus of the adults on campus.

Table 5.4 focuses on the core reason we have schools—teaching and learning. Teaching is not a zero sum game of labeling and sorting kids into who should and should not have access to equitable educational opportunities. Culturally proficient school leaders ensure that grade-level and department meetings, faculty meetings, learning community meetings, and professional development sessions are organized in such a way that educators learn from and with one another about the diversity of the community they serve and the manner in which successful learning techniques and curricular adaptations provide for equitable approaches to working with students.

The Pine Hills' Learning Community

Principal:	This may come as a surprise to the two of you since you have been conscientious educators all along, but Table 5.4 represents a great shift since I first became a vice principal.
SLT Teacher:	How do you mean?
Principal:	Well, just a few years ago my success was measured by whether or not "I could keep the lid on my school." As I attended conferences around the area and at the national level, I saw other administrators who had the same expectations placed on them. Now, the accountability movement has changed all that and we are now placed in the role

	of needing to know more about teaching and learning. To be honest with you, many of my colleagues are struggling mightily!
Emilia:	I can imagine! But, isn't it interesting—"keep the lid on!" Wow, that says it all. No wonder there is so much resistance to the changes that we are discussing.
Principal:	True, but I believe that as we combine this focus on teaching and learning with the earlier issues of assumptions, etc., it may not be all that difficult.
Emilia:	Oh, I agree. One of the things I learned at the STA session was the accountability movement, if it has done nothing else, has provided the opportunity to discuss student achievement in ways that we have not before.
SLT Teacher:	Well, as you know, I was one of the early resistors of the Learning Community concept. Seemed like a monumental waste of time and energy, but I am now ready to admit I was wrong. It is about my and our willingness to learn, in this case, what it takes to be successful with kids from this community.
Principal:	Yes, for me, too. I and we have to be diligent in everything we do to keep our and our students' learning our central focus.

Dialogic Questions for You and Your Colleagues

In what ways do you and your school hold teaching and learning as your central focus? What do you want to learn in the next two years? In what ways will you benefit? In what ways does what you want to learn benefit the students in your school? In what ways can you contribute to the learning of your colleagues? Please use the space below to record your personal thoughts and the insights you gain from dialogue with colleagues? Please use the space below to record your personal thoughts and the insights you gain from dialogue with colleagues.

_____

_____

_____

_____

Belief 5: Leaders Promote a Sense of Curiosity About the Interrelationship of Curriculum, Instruction, Shared Vision for Student Learning, and Social Justice

It may seem strange to have the final table be the one that introduces "vision," but there is good reason. We position this table last because the foundation for a truly informed vision and mission rests on knowing the community in authentic ways. Information garnered from the previous tables provides substance for developing vision and mission statements that intend to respond to the needs of your community. Vision is informed when school leaders recognize their assumptions about the communities they serve, have a palpable sense of the community, are aware of the structural inequities that exist in the large community, and have a commitment to equity.

Table 5.5 shows the alignment of

- The standards for professional leaders—shared vision for learning,
- The essential elements—managing dynamics of difference and institutionalizing cultural knowledge, with
- The belief statement about poverty—curiosity about the interrelationship of curriculum and instruction, mission, and high expectations.

Table 5.5 Alignment of Professional Standards of Improving Teaching With Belief Statements About Poverty and Essential Elements

Professional Standards for Educational Leaders	Belief Statements for Schools Serving Communities of Poverty	Essential Elements of Cultural Competence
Education leaders ensure the achievement of all students by guiding the development and implementation of a shared vision of learning, strong organizational mission, and high expectations for every student.	Leaders promote a sense of curiosity about the interrelationship of the curriculum, the instruction, student learning, and social justice.	Manage the Dynamics of Difference and Institutionalize Cultural Knowledge

Education leaders begin the development of a shared vision by examining their own assumptions and beliefs. "Do I believe that every student can learn at high levels? Do I believe that collaboration and distributed leadership are effective ways to work?" As they begin the work of forging a vision, effective leaders use data to inform and direct the school community's efforts to improvement. They create an all-inclusive tent that demands diverse perspectives and the voice of every group as they move forward in forging the school's vision. They advocate for a variety of strategies as they develop and implement the shared vision.

Literature on leadership in the last quarter of the 20th century showed the development of vision and mission statements as an important step for organizations (Heifetz, 1994; Senge et al., 2000). Emulating the practices of businesses, preK–12 schools regularly develop vision and statements as part of their accreditation processes. Words such as, "becoming an active and contributing member of a democratic society" appears in almost every school mission statement that we encounter. However, the nascent accountability measures in mandated requirements such as NCLB (2002) requiring schools to disaggregate achievement data for their demographic groups has made it clear that many schools and school districts are not succeeding in meeting their lofty vision and mission statements.

Structures within schools that sort and select students into lower and higher learning groups have not served the needs of low-income and impoverished students in equitable fashion (Lemann, 1999). Analysis of achievement data indicates what many have known for over 30 years: Having full access to equitable educational opportunities afforded by democratic societies was not happening for students from low-income, impoverished communities (Perie, Moran, & Lutkus, 2005).

Educational leaders gather, organize, and present data that help us understand what we are dealing with as it relates to students in poverty. The Educational Testing Service published a report in 2009, "Parsing the Achievement Gap," (Barton & Coley, 2009) that has identified differences in School Factors, Home and School Connections, and Before and Beyond School and gathered data in 16 areas where students in poverty differ from the balance of the student population. While these are informative for education leaders, they should not be seen as insurmountable obstacles to student achievement. This study is a continuation of one done in 2003. It finds that presently not much has changed for these students. Berliner (2009) believes gaps persist because our focus on only the school is too narrow. He cites a number of areas—health care, nutrition, violence prevention, housing, mobility, and absenteeism—as important factors as we address student achievement. In England, Every Child Matters (http://www.every childmatters.gov.uk/) is similar to No Child Left Behind, but there are components within the school that address some of Berliner's concerns about non-school factors that affect achievement. As we continue to address the concerns of student achievement, it's important that we continue to promote, not only within the ranks of education and educators but at every level and corner of government, the realization that grade-level academic achievement is the best sign of a healthy child, a healthy community, and the most effective way to ensure the future of our democratic way of life.

Curiosity and vision are brought together in Table 5.5. The forces of vision, mission, and social justice can impel educators and schools to inquire about the limitations and strengths of curriculum and instruction in ways that serve the needs of low-income and impoverished communities.

The Pine Hills' Learning Community

SLT Teacher: So, I'll bet we can't just dust off the document we slaved over for our recent regional accreditation and use it as a road map, can we?

Principal: As valuable as I think that process was, I don't think we got near out of it what we should have.

Emilia: Of course, we can always second-guess ourselves, but two important things came out of that for me. First, our core group of parents was steadfastly in support of PHHS. Second, I was surprised by how many of our colleagues wanted the school to do well.

SLT Teacher: Of course; who wants to be on a losing team?

Emilia: Those are nice words, but our academic image is poor and we still get teachers and administrators who see this school as an intermediate stop on their way to better jobs!

Principal: It begins with us!

SLT Teacher: What do you mean by that?

Emilia: Let me take a stab at it. As I look back over these five tables, if we want this school to succeed, what are we willing to do to make it happen? We are not talking rocket science here. We know that we have limited impact on these students', parents', and guardians' social and economic experiences, but we certainly have the capacity to make a difference. We know these kids are bright and capable. Our limitation is that we need to learn how to be successful. The onus is on us.

SLT Teacher: I remember in my undergraduate program reading the *Foxfire* books about a teacher in rural northern Georgia who used the kids' own context to teach them. His value was the kids' capacity to learn, and it was his responsibility to organize learning experiences for them. Of course, in doing so he was organizing his own learning experiences.

Principal: I watched a movie recently about a teacher in an urban district in California who did something similar.

Emilia: So, what are our next steps?

In Chapter 4 we advocated for examining the assumptions that guide the practice of classroom teachers and those who support them. The belief statements introduced by Emilia in this chapter build on knowing our assumptions and being able and willing to align our espoused values with the Guiding Principles of Cultural Proficiency. Doing so serves as powerful indicators of the core values of the educators at Pine Hills High School. The vignettes demonstrated the manner in which formal and non-formal school leaders discuss, explore, and communicate their shared views of education, assumptions about students from low-income and impoverished communities, and the manner in which they view and interact with the community that surrounds the school. Chapter 6 is devoted to an examination of policy development that serves low-income and impoverished communities.

Going Deeper

So, what are your next steps?

_____

_____

_____

_____

_____

_____

_____

_____

6

Policy Development to Ensure and Support Teaching and Learning

Tackling tough problems—problems that require an evolution of values—is the end of leadership; getting that work done is its essence.

—Ron Heifetz, 1994, p. 26

Getting Centered

Maple View School District has been experiencing a slow, steady change in demographics in recent years. The change in student socioeconomic composition accelerated about the same time that national and state guidelines emerged requiring local school districts to examine current educational practices in unprecedented ways. As an example, Superintendent Sam Brewer had known of the underachievement of English learners and low-income students for some time. Though sensitive to the fact that individual school and district scores were high, some of his key administrators and school board trustees felt little pressure to address the issue of "sub-group" test scores. Superintendent Brewer decided to use state and federal mandates as a theme for his upcoming leadership retreat.

No Child Left Behind (NCLB) and corresponding state mandates now require districts to address the needs of all demographic groups of students. The growth of English learners and of low-income students exacerbated the situation and had leaders of Maple View concerned. Their work with the tools of cultural proficiency had been helpful, other than the fact that some school leaders chafed at the notion that they had privilege and entitlement that made them responsible, if not for the historical inequities, most certainly for the current situation. Superintendent Brewer prided himself as being a champion of diversity and was disconcerted that some of his administrators and trustees were rankled when the topic of privilege and entitlement presented in professional development sessions.

The vignette that follows portrays the policy-level considerations Superintendent Brewer undertakes with the support and assistance of his coach/consultant.

Brewer:	To be sure, some of my administrators and a couple of trustees are incensed at the implication that they haven't done all that they can to educate all students to high levels. I am proud of the fact that I have always been committed to all students learning and getting my fellow policymakers to get beyond feeling blamed and getting on to the business of having policies and practices to ensure equitable education is our challenge.
Coach:	What is it about the session that triggered this reaction and pronouncement of being blamed?
Brewer:	The voices I heard were with you when we discussed the need to embrace the guiding principles as core values for the district. The same voices were with you when you involved us in an activity to chart our comments and practices and to array them along the Cultural Proficiency Continuum. And, they state they were with you when we delved into the essential elements as standards for educator behaviors and school district values. But, this privilege and entitlement piece went way too far for some of them! In fact, one particularly strong voice expressed she has been a successful educator, a teacher, and an administrator, and for you or anyone to suggest that she and others have been ignoring part of

their jobs is completely unacceptable! Another voice expressed that you, as our consultant, don't know what it is like working in a heavily impacted school.

Coach: Superintendent Brewer, did your colleagues recall our first session when I asked, "How many people in the room believe that classism has existed historically in our community and that it still persists?"

Brewer: No, it didn't come up in our debriefing session. However, I remember it clearly and, if you recall, predicted it would be a stumbling block for many of my colleagues. Let's talk about how to proceed. Our assistant superintendent for curriculum and instruction would like to join our conversation; is that okay with you? He is struggling with this concept of privilege and entitlement.

Administrator: [Enters the superintendent's conference room] I am sure the superintendent has let you know that your presentation on privilege and entitlement threw me off kilter. However, I do want to understand. Whether I agree or not is immaterial at this time.

Coach: I appreciate this opportunity for dialogue. Maybe you will remember, my next comment was "if people are not afforded rights and privileges based on their membership in a socioeconomic group, then it stands to reason that others gain those rights and privileges."

Administrator: Yes, of course. I also remember your using voting as an analogy. If one person is denied the right to vote, then it increases the value for those who do vote. But, this new privilege and entitlement stuff has crossed the line into meddling! But you are inferring that I have somehow limited the rights of others intentionally.

Coach: How do you mean?

Administrator: I feel blamed and accused, that is what!

Coach: First, please recognize that your feelings may be an important cue to your own deeper learning.

Administrator: How so?

Coach: Because the accountability procedures now in place are making you feel blamed that low-income students have not been given a fair shake. Am I correct about that? Isn't it true that the Title I student has never performed at high levels in your school? Haven't you known about this deficiency long before NCLB?

Administrator: Well, I guess so. I have always done all that I could do, and. . . .

Coach: All that you could do . . . ? And now those in charge of state and federal accountability measures are saying that "all you have done in the past" is not enough. Isn't that right?

Administrator: You're damned right that is the issue! Why don't they come here and try to teach these kids?!

Coach: Are you ready for the "deeper learning" that I described during our professional development session?

Administrator: What do you mean?

Coach: You are on the verge of the deeper personal learning if you are ready to move beyond feeling maligned and to embrace the guiding principles as core values for you and for this district. If you are willing to see the essential elements as standards for developing and adapting district policies and practices based in the belief that students' culture, in this case poverty, can be the basis on which you can build an effective educational program.

Administrator: Okay, okay, it is beginning to resonate in a way that I can actually "hear"!

Coach: Say more about what you are connecting?

Administrator: Your constant refrain in our PD sessions has been "change is an inside-out process." The students are who they are and it is up to us to figure out how to teach them. I hate to admit it, but I have been under the delusion that it was either a "teacher issue" or that there was some magic to low-income students' learning that we would discover. I have to be as involved in the change process as much as any classroom teacher, parent, or student in this district.

Brewer: Precisely! None of us can be observers of the change process that entails our being effective in the education of all students, in particular those from our low-income or impoverished communities.

Reflection

What thoughts and reactions occur to you as you reflect on the conversation with Superintendent Brewer and the consultant? In what ways do school and district policy support or restrain educational improvement? Please use the space provided to record your responses.

_____

_____

_____

_____

The Intent of This Chapter

This chapter is guided by the following questions:

- In what ways do the tools of cultural proficiency guide personal reflection and dialogue among educators?
- In what ways do policymakers respond to questions seeking to explore big-picture needs?
- In what ways do policymakers influence what educators need to learn to be successful with students from low-income and impoverished communities?

Policymakers serving the needs of students from low-income and impoverished communities cannot shirk their responsibility in leading learning for serving students. The examination of assumptions that guide policy development and implementation is the same as for any other educator. Examining assumptions is fundamental to developing and implementing policies and practices that have the expressed intent of educating children and youth in a manner that honors who they are and that results in their being able to make informed choices to guide their lives.

Who Are the Policymakers?

We define policymakers as those who have legal authority derived from provincial or state authorities to guide school districts (also referred to as school boards in some provinces of Canada). Policymakers include school board members and trustees who are elected or appointed to their roles. Superintendents and other line administrators who have formal, designated authority from provincial or state and via local board or trustee policies and actions are policymakers. It is also important to note there are individuals in the school districts and school communities who exercise informal authority through meeting expectations of trustworthiness, ability, or civility (Heifetz, 1994).

Culturally Proficient Policy Development in Two Steps

Culturally proficient policy development involves the same two components used for any change in personal or professional behavior or school practice: (1) consideration of supporting values or policies, accompanied by (2) change in behavior or practices.

Step 1

Deep consideration of the guiding principles and the essential elements as described in Chapter 3 are necessary for the educational leader who is authentically interested in meeting the academic and social needs of all students, and in particular, students from low socioeconomic backgrounds. We know of no shortcuts to this personal and organizational self-examination. In fact, we believe it to be a healthy process for all involved. The guiding principles and essential elements are beneficial in these ways:

- The Guiding Principles of Cultural Proficiency (Table 3.2) serve as personal and organizational core values to guide educational leaders as they address the barriers of educator and institutional expressions of classism that obstruct student achievement.
- The Essential Elements of Cultural Competence serve as standards for individual values and behaviors and organizational policies and practices (Tables 3.4 and 6.1–6.3). The essential elements build on the value for culture implicit in the guiding principles and, thereby, enable educational leaders to view students from low-income backgrounds as arriving at school

with experiences on which educators can build constructive, educational experiences that serve the needs of students.

Step 2

Intentionally engage in reflection and dialogue as a means of developing and modeling the importance of serving the needs of low-income students.

- Reflection is when we "talk" with ourselves (either ourselves as a leader or our organization as a cultural entity that perpetuates inequitable policies and practices—knowingly or unknowingly has the same impact on the underserved, therefore, not knowing cannot be an excuse). Later in this chapter we present the types of questions that educators seeking to be culturally proficient can use to deepen their own understanding and to use in guiding their schools and district policymakers. Tables 6.1 and 6.2 and the accompanying narratives serve to foster the creation of a "mindset" of inclusion, equity, and empowerment.
- Dialogue is when we engage peers, colleagues, and community members in a manner to understand their daily lives, such as the
  - Impact of inequitable access to health care, affordable housing, and jobs on low-income communities.
  - Impact of changing behaviors and underlying values by educators who have not been held accountable for the education of children and youth from low-income communities.
  - Impact of changing policies and practices by a school system that has heretofore not been held accountable for the education of children and youth from low-income communities.
  - Impact of the racial predictability of the highest-performing students and lowest-performing students in identifying which students are successful and not successful in our schools; the gap between many racial groups.

- Table 6.3 provides guiding questions that facilitate dialogue to develop mindsets among educators and policymakers that foster equity, inclusiveness, and empowerment.

Educators and educational policymakers who engage in deep reflection and dialogue to better serve the needs of historically underserved students are involved in their own learning. Likewise, these educators are engaged in leading the learning of their educator and policymaker colleagues. Such educators are intentional in seeking the big picture of what needs to be accomplished in their school or district and their role to guide and support the learning of school leaders and policymakers.

As you may recall, in Chapter 3 we describe "adapting to diversity" as a guiding principle, a core value, of cultural proficiency. Prominent educational researchers and theorists have recognized adaptive leadership as fundamental to the development of leaders committed to the education of all students (Garmston & Wellman, 1999; Heifetz, 1994; Hilliard, 1991; Senge et al., 2000). The current accountability movement provides the impetus for our following through on what Michael Fullan (2003) referred to as our moral imperative, namely the education of all students.

Adaptive Leadership

Heifetz's (1994) notion of adaptive leadership seamlessly connects to the Essential Elements of Cultural Competence—assessing cultural knowledge, valuing diversity, managing the dynamics of difference, adapting to diversity, and institutionalizing cultural knowledge:

> . . . leadership is oriented by the task of doing adaptive work. . . . We need a view of leadership that provides a practical orientation so that we can evaluate events and action in process, without waiting for outcomes. . . . a strategy of leadership to accomplish adaptive work accounts for several conditions and values that are consonant with the demands of a democratic society. In addition to reality testing, these include respecting conflict, negotiation, and a diversity of views within the community; increasing community cohesion; developing norms of responsibility-taking, learning, and innovation; and keeping social distress within a bearable range. (p. 26)

Leaders must be reflective *and* active. School leaders engaged in meeting the needs of all students, and in particular students from low-income or impoverished communities, need to be actively engaged in the day-to-day issues of running schools (i.e., being active) and, concomitantly, holding a perspective that provides for a larger view of who is and who is not being appropriately educated (i.e., being reflective). We have adapted the work of Heifetz (1994) and Senge et al. (2000) and created a series of questions to guide school leaders in developing policies and practices to equitably serve students from low-income or impoverished communities.

Table 6.1 provides reflective questions that provide a *big-picture perspective* through diagnosing the nature of student under-education

Table 6.1   Reflective Questions to Guide Educational Leaders in Culturally Proficient Big-Picture Policy Development

Essential Elements of Cultural Competence	Questions to Guide Big-Picture Perspective
Assess Cultural Knowledge	What barriers exist within the district in responding to the new requirements to be accountable for the education of low-income students? Is it the current accountability movement or something deeper?
	What values of our educator colleagues are being challenged with regard to educating children and youth from low-income backgrounds?
	In what ways are we in the policymaking leadership group mirroring the problem dynamics in the school-community?
Value Diversity	In what ways might current policy or practice be challenged with regard to educating children and youth from low-income backgrounds?
	What perspectives and interests have I, and others, come to represent to various segments of the community that are now in conflict?
	In what ways are we expressing confidence in the capacity of the school and the community it serves?

and the manner in which under-education is reflected in the attitudes held by educators toward children and youth from low-income backgrounds.

We refer to the "big picture" as a culturally proficient perspective in that it holds high regard for students' cultures. The questions are aligned with the Essential Elements of Cultural Competence. Your responses to the questions will provide guidance to understanding how historical policies and practices, whether intentional or not, have led to disparities in student achievement in your school district.

Reflection

What thoughts occur to you as you read the questions? What kinds of insights or observations do you think answers to the questions might provide to you? Take another look at Table 6.1 and note the essential elements. What thoughts or reactions occur to you? Please use the space below to record your comments.

_____

_____

_____

_____

_____

_____

_____

Table 6.2 poses reflective questions to guide understanding levels of challenging prevailing practices and learning that the school community can tolerate. Your response to these questions will lead to greater understanding of the forces that have supported and resisted change in your school district. Thoughtful consideration of the questions and your responses will provide an ever deeper understanding of the organizational culture of your school district. In this way you become a student of your own school or system and identify and study its culture. The organizational culture will become transparent and you will discern the historical practices and policies that well serve the privileged students and underserve chronically under-achieving students.

Table 6.2   Reflective Questions to Guide Educational Leaders in Understanding
Challenges to Prevailing Practice and Learning in Culturally Proficient
Policy Development

Essential Elements of Cultural Competence	Questions to Understand Challenges to Prevailing Practice and Learning a School Can Tolerate
Institutionalize Cultural Knowledge	What are the characteristic responses to challenges to prevailing practice—confusion about future direction, the presence of externally imposed changes, disorientation in regard to role relationships, internal conflict, or creation of new norms of behavior? _____ _____ _____
Assess Cultural Knowledge	When in the past have challenges to prevailing practice appeared to reach a breaking point—where the social system in a school or in the district began to engage in self-destructive behavior, like sabotaging efforts to improve education for historically marginalized groups of students or diversifying the faculty? _____ _____ _____
Manage the Dynamics of Difference	What actions by policymakers traditionally have restored balance in the district? What mechanisms to restore balance are currently within my control, given my or our authority? _____ _____ _____
	What breakthrough questions can I pose that will prompt thinking and action on behalf of historically marginalized students in this school system? _____ _____ _____

Reflection

The questions in Table 6.2 guide you into deeper consideration of
your school or school system. What thoughts or reactions occur as
you read the questions? What do you see as the risks and benefits of
asking these questions of yourself and your colleagues? Please use
the space below to record your comments.

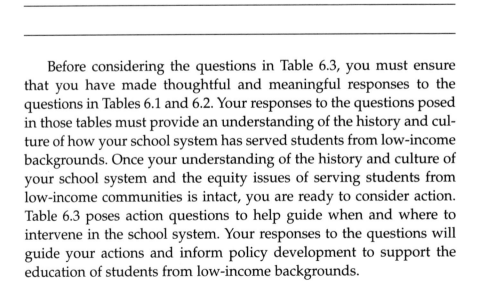

Before considering the questions in Table 6.3, you must ensure
that you have made thoughtful and meaningful responses to the
questions in Tables 6.1 and 6.2. Your responses to the questions posed
in those tables must provide an understanding of the history and culture of how your school system has served students from low-income
backgrounds. Once your understanding of the history and culture of
your school system and the equity issues of serving students from
low-income communities is intact, you are ready to consider action.
Table 6.3 poses action questions to help guide when and where to
intervene in the school system. Your responses to the questions will
guide your actions and inform policy development to support the
education of students from low-income backgrounds.

Table 6.3   Action Questions to Guide Educational Leaders in Intervening for Culturally Proficient Policy Development

Essential Elements of Cultural Competence	Questions to Help Guide When and Where to Intervene in the School System
Assess Cultural Knowledge	What are the work and work avoidance patterns particular to this school-community? In what ways do educators and policymakers put energy into historically successful activities? In what ways have educators avoided issues that underlie achievement gaps?
Adapt to Diversity	What does the current pattern of work avoidance indicate about the nature and difficulty of the present adaptive challenge and the various work issues that it comprises?
	What clues do the authority figures provide?
Institutionalize Cultural Knowledge	Which of these issues are ripe? What are the options for tackling the ripe issues, or for ripening an issue that has not fastened in people's minds?

Reflection

What might be some of the risks and benefits to asking the questions in Table 6.3? How do you think your colleagues would react to the questions? What might be the reactions of community members who have been historically marginalized once they know these questions are guiding actions by the school? Please use the space below to record your responses.

_____

_____

_____

_____

   We began this book by stating the purpose to be about how educators reach deep within ourselves to care enough to learn how to teach children from low-income and impoverished backgrounds. To do so is to intentionally embrace an asset-based perspective when viewing and working with our students and families from low-income and impoverished communities. We have endeavored to provide ideas and suggestions for how to engage with colleagues collectively to reach within our schools and school systems to create the conditions in which children and youth from impoverished backgrounds achieve at high levels.

Going Deeper

What do you think? How will you proceed in your role as an educator in service to students and families from low-income and impoverished communities?

_____

_____

_____

_____

_____

_____

PART III

A Call to Action

The final chapter of this book invites and supports you in addressing the two major roles educators presented in Part I— as individual educators and as members of school systems:

- Through reflection we reach deeply within ourselves and care enough to learn how to teach children from low-income and impoverished backgrounds.
- Through dialogue we engage with our colleagues to reach within our schools and school systems to create conditions in which children and youth from low-income and impoverished backgrounds achieve at high levels.

By this point in the book, you know of the centrality of reflection and dialogue to creating culturally proficient classrooms and schools. Responding to the academic and social needs of students from low-income and impoverished conditions is a moral responsibility of our schools in Canada and the United States. As discussed in Chapter 1, being successful in such communities means recognizing the structural and systemic nature of poverty in society, but focusing our attention on what we do during the time students are in classrooms and on campus. Throughout this book, we have made the case that culturally proficient approaches begin with an examination of our assumptions about students as learners. Reflection and dialogue guide examination of assumptions that block our effectiveness in working within low-income and impoverished communities.

Chapter 7 provides prompts to guide your personal reflection and dialogue with colleagues. You are invited to bring forward your learning and insights from previous chapters, to examine your role as a professional educator, and to intentionally set goals for your own learning in service of your students. We close the book with a quote from Margaret Wheatley that, for us, speaks to the power of conversation—whether reflective or dialogic.

7

A Call to Action

The Time Is Now

Our Invitation to You

We opened this book describing cultural proficiency as an asset-based approach to education. Our premise was that students from low-income and impoverished communities are fully capable of learning, and it is our role to educate them. We shared a related premise that we educators are knowledgeable of the technical aspects of our roles as educators, whether as a teacher, a counselor, an administrator, or a policymaker. Then, we presented cultural proficiency as a means to developing a relationship with our students and their communities.

Our invitation is for you to use this chapter to think about your thinking—to return to some of the writing and thinking you did in previous chapters and to organize your thinking in terms of continuous improvement for you and for your school or school system.

Personal and Organizational Change

We introduced Dilts's (1994) model for personal and organizational change in Part I and noted its alignment with cultural proficiency's inside-out approach to change. Table 7.1 is repeated from the Part I introduction. You may recall the premise of Dilts's nested levels is change that occurs at one level affects each subsequent level. Guiding

Table 7.1   Cultural Proficiency's Inside-Out Approach to Personal and
Organizational Change Aligned With Dilts's Nested Levels

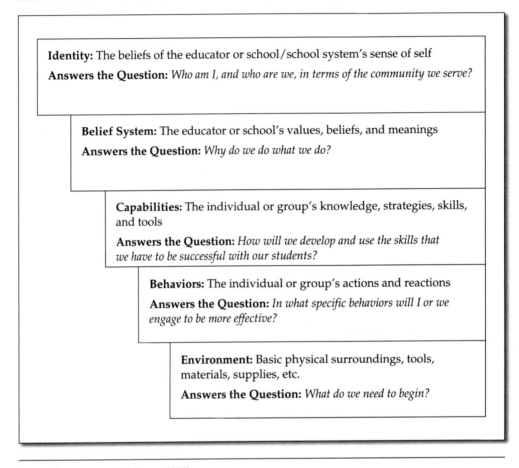

Identity: The beliefs of the educator or school/school system's sense of self

Answers the Question: *Who am I, and who are we, in terms of the community we serve?*

Belief System: The educator or school's values, beliefs, and meanings

Answers the Question: *Why do we do what we do?*

Capabilities: The individual or group's knowledge, strategies, skills, and tools

Answers the Question: *How will we develop and use the skills that we have to be successful with our students?*

Behaviors: The individual or group's actions and reactions

Answers the Question: *In what specific behaviors will I or we engage to be more effective?*

Environment: Basic physical surroundings, tools, materials, supplies, etc.

Answers the Question: *What do we need to begin?*

Source: Garmston and Wellman (1999).

your attention to the two lowest "nests" of Dilts's model, "behaviors and environment" is where change often begins for schools. This is most often the case with change that is externally motivated such as with No Child Left Behind or other compliance-driven change.

Our argument is that compliance-driven change too often is limited to the specific mandate or demographic population. In fact, much of the educational change that has occurred in the last 50 years in service of female students, students of color, students with different abilities, and students from low-income or impoverished communities has been initiated by compliance with federal or state mandates. Our position is that effective leadership, whether the teacher within the classroom or leaders within the school or school systems, has the opportunity to assume the moral responsibility to provide for the educational needs of all students.

Dilts's model and the tools of cultural proficiency provide a template and set of tools to chart the continuous improvement changes you seek to make in your own educational practice as well as that of your school or school system. In the pages that follow, you are invited to use this chapter to do your thinking. This may be your personal journey and/or it may be a journey you are taking with colleagues.

Your Personal Journey: Issues of Low-Income and Impoverished Communities

This section is designed for you to bring forward your work in the earlier chapters and to summarize your learning. For purposes of planning, we are asking you to consider your learning in two domains: as your own personal journey, and as an educator working with students and parents or guardians in low-income or impoverished communities.

Your Personal Journey

This section is designed for you to bring forward your work in the earlier chapters and to summarize your learning. Following are questions and space for your responses:

Describe what have you learned, or affirmed, about your attitudes toward people from low-income and impoverished communities.

_____

_____

_____

_____

What might be some ways schools as middle class entities limit their effectiveness in service of low-income and impoverished communities?

_____

_____

_____

_____

What might be some ways educators limit their effectiveness when working with students and parents or guardians from low-income or impoverished communities?

_____

_____

_____

_____

What support factors exist for you? For your community?

_____

_____

_____

_____

Describe ways in which the four families followed in this book resonated in your personal or professional life.

_____

_____

_____

_____

In what ways do the tools of cultural proficiency provide insight to you as a person living in a diverse society?

_____

_____

_____

_____

Your Professional Journey

With this section you have the opportunity to examine your role as an educator as well as being a member of a school and school system.

Describe asset-based approaches and how they differ from deficit-based approaches.

_____

_____

_____

_____

Think about your role as an educator (teacher, leader, and/or policy-maker) and describe your areas of confidence about educating students from low-income or impoverished communities.

_____

_____

_____

_____

Continue thinking about your role as an educator (teacher, leader, and/or policymaker) and describe what you need to learn about serving the educational needs of students from low-income and impoverished communities.

_____

_____

_____

_____

Next Steps: Being Intentional

The usefulness of this book may be measured by what you commit to doing. To this point, your personal learning has been guided by your reflective responses to questions throughout this book or by the dialogic responses of you and your colleagues. The following questions can be used for personal, professional planning, or in community with colleagues.

What do you want for your students from low-income or impoverished communities that is within your areas of influence?

_____

_____

_____

_____

_____

_____

What are you willing to commit to doing over the next three years to realize the goal(s) you have set in service of your students from low-income or impoverished communities?

_____

_____

_____

_____

What are you willing to commit to doing over the next year to realize the goal(s) you have set in service of your students from low-income or impoverished communities?

_____

_____

_____

_____

What are you willing to commit to over the next week (yes, seven days!) to realize the goal(s) you have set in service of your students from low-income or impoverished communities?

_____

_____

_____

_____

A Conversation That Matters

You picked up and have been reading this book because you care about the education of all students, in particular the students who are the focus of this book—students from low-income and impoverished communities. You have kept reading and responding to the prompts throughout this book because you want to improve your craft. Most likely, you believe that our democracies have the capacity to be inclusive of people from a wide variety of socioeconomic and cultural groups. You want to be part of a group that solves problems.

After the horrific events of September 11, 2001, Margaret Wheatley, a noted expert on community and organizational learning, was concerned that our society would become increasingly fractured and would spin out of control. The education of children and youth has been marginalized, for too long, in our countries, yet there is abundant research and literature cited throughout this book to demonstrate that these students are capable of learning and that it is our job to learn how best to teach them. We, the authors, have emphasized the central nature of personal reflection and collegial dialogue in learning how to be of service to students from low-income and impoverished communities. We close this book with a passage from Wheatley's 2002 book, *Turning to One Another: Simple Conversations to Restore Hope to the Future*:

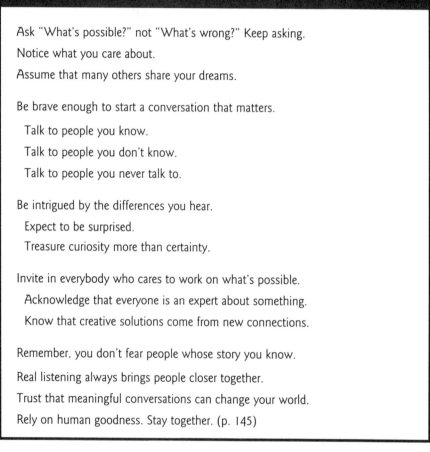

There Is No Power Greater Than a Community Discovering What It Cares About

Ask "What's possible?" not "What's wrong?" Keep asking.

Notice what you care about.

Assume that many others share your dreams.

Be brave enough to start a conversation that matters.

  Talk to people you know.

  Talk to people you don't know.

  Talk to people you never talk to.

Be intrigued by the differences you hear.

  Expect to be surprised.

  Treasure curiosity more than certainty.

Invite in everybody who cares to work on what's possible.

  Acknowledge that everyone is an expert about something.

  Know that creative solutions come from new connections.

Remember, you don't fear people whose story you know.

Real listening always brings people closer together.

Trust that meaningful conversations can change your world.

Rely on human goodness. Stay together. (p. 145)

We are pleased with your interest in this work and look forward to learning from and with you. As you experience successes and challenges in service of students and their parents or guardians from low-income and impoverished communities, we would enjoy hearing from you. Our commitment is, through this medium and others, to share our successes and what we are learning from our challenges.

Randy (randallblindsey@gmail.com)

Michelle (mskarns@pacbell.net)

Keith (keith.myatt@gmail.com)

Resource A

Cultural Proficiency
Conceptual Framework

The Five Essential Elements of Cultural Competence

Serve as standards for personal, professional values and behaviors, as well as organizational policies and practices:

- Assessing cultural knowledge
- Valuing diversity
- Managing the dynamics of difference
- Adapting to diversity
- Institutionalizing cultural knowledge

Informs

The Cultural Proficiency Continuum portrays people and organizations who possess the knowledge, skills, and moral bearing to distinguish among healthy and unhealthy practices as represented by different worldviews:

Unhealthy Practices

Informs

- Cultural destructiveness
- Cultural incapacity
- Cultural blindness

Differing Worldviews

Healthy Practices

- Cultural precompetence
- Cultural competence
- Cultural proficiency

Informs

Resolving the tension to do what is socially just within our diverse society leads people and organizations to view selves in terms Unhealthy and Healthy.

Barriers to Cultural Proficiency

Serve as personal, professional, and institutional impediments to moral and just service to a diverse society by

- being resistant to change,
- being unaware of the need to adapt,
- not acknowledging systemic oppression, and
- benefiting from a sense of privilege and entitlement.

Ethical Tension

Guiding Principles of Cultural Proficiency

Provide a moral framework for conducting one's self and organization in an ethical fashion by believing the following:

- Culture is a predominant force in society.
- People are served in varying degrees by the dominant culture.
- People have individual and group identities.
- Diversity within cultures is vast and significant.
- Each cultural group has unique cultural needs.
- The best of both worlds enhances the capacity of all.
- The family, as defined by each culture, is the primary system of support in the education of children.
- School systems must recognize that marginalized populations have to be at least bicultural and that this status creates a distinct set of issues to which the system must be equipped to respond.
- Inherent in cross-cultural interactions are dynamics that must be acknowledged, adjusted to, and accepted.

Source: Cultural Proficiency: A Manual for School Leaders, 3rd ed. (2009), by Randall B. Lindsey, Kikanza Nuri-Robins, and Raymond D. Terrell.

Resource B

State Teachers' Association Retreat Script

State Teachers' Association

Saturday and Sunday

8:30 a.m. to 4 p.m.

Theme: Changing the Conversation

Saturday

Slide	Time	Activity	Materials or Equipment
	8:00–8:30	Coffee	
1–11	8:30–10:00	Introductions and Session Overview • Begin PowerPoint (PPT) • Creating Conditions o Turning to One Another Reading 1 o What's in a Name? o Cultural Perceptions Activity	• Projector for PowerPoint • PPT presentation • *Manual*, 217 • *Manual*, 214
12	10:00–10:15	Browse Through *Manual* • Table of Contents o Text o Resources • Read Overview of the four tools—read pages 4–7	• *Manual*, 4–7
	10:15–10:30	Break	

Slide	Time	Activity	Materials or Equipment
13–17	10:30–11:00	Guiding Principles of Cultural Proficiency: Core Values of Model • Scan pages 98–108 • Name 5 Things Activity • Beliefs statement • Bring attention to activities in *Manual*	• Name 5 Things, *Manual*, 186–187
18	11:00–11:45	Telling Your Story • Brief introductory lecturette • Diverse groups of 4 people • In turn, each person picks a cell and tells a story of events in their lives (20–30 minutes) • Debrief using questions, page 168	• *Manual*, 169
19		Culturally Proficient Professional • Read *Manual*, page 21 • Table talk: "Aha's and connections being made?"	• *Manual*, 21
	12:00–1:00	Lunch	
20	1:00–1:15	Getting Centered Activity: Paired Fluency • Begin with lineup (birthdays, place of birth?)	
21–23	1:15–2:00	Cultural Proficiency Continuum: Framing the Conversation • Continue PPT Presentation • Sticky Notes Activity • "Words"	• Newsprint and sticky notes • *Manual*, 275–280
24–26	2:00–2:45	The Five Essential Elements of Cultural Competence • Cultural Competence Self-Assessment Activity ○ Personal Focus to complete instrument ○ Small group discussion–areas of strength, future growth, surprises, or insights ○ Large group discussion–lessons learned about elements as standards for behaviors and policies • "Changing the Conversation" from *Schools* book	• PPT • *Manual*, 295–296
	2:45–3:00	Break	
27–28	3:00–3:45	Barriers to Cultural Proficiency: Issues of Resistance to Change • Left-hand store analogy (*others* make changes) • Implications for oppressed • Implications for those who are privileged and entitled by current practices	
29–32	3:45–4:00	Closing • Journaling • With the Continuum in mind, pay attention to the comments you hear from colleagues over the next few days.	• *Manual*, 182–183

Sunday

Slide	Time	Activity	Materials or Equipment
	8:00–8:30	Coffee	
33–34	8:30–9:00	Checking-In Activity	• PPT
35–37	9:00–10:00	Reading • Pages 3–18	• *Inquiry*, 3–18
	10:00–10:15	Break	

38–39	10:15–11:00	Rubrics
		• Read *Inquiry*, 73–79
		• Respond to Reflection, 79
		
		Curriculum and Instruction or Assessment and Accountability Rubric from *Culturally Proficient Inquiry*
		
		• Given our discussions last session and this morning of the Guiding Principles and Essential Elements:
		  o Have participants, singly or in groups, locate their school(s) along the continuum for each of the essential elements.
		  o Have participants speculate where they think their teacher colleagues might place the school for each of the elements.
		  o Respond to this question: Within our current school processes, where and how do we move the conversation and decisions that will result in movement toward proficiency?
			• *Inquiry*, 73–79
			• C & I or Assessment Rubrics, pages 81–87

40	11:00–12:00	Barrier and Breakthrough Questions • Read handout • Organize into teams to discuss (dyads, etc.) Table 1.2 • I will model 1 or 2 with them • Back to teams to work on Table 1.3 • Group discussion	
	12:00–1:00	Lunch	
41	1:00–3:30	Your School Data	
42–43	3:30–4:00	Closing • Voices That Resonate, *Manual*, 230 • With the Continuum in mind, pay attention to the comments you hear from colleagues over the next few days. • Wheatley Reading	• *Manual*, 230 • Wheatley, *Turning to One Another*

Slide	Time	Activity	Materials or Equipment

Materials and Equipment

- Handout packet to include
  - ○ PowerPoint
  - ○ Give One, Get One Handout
  - ○ Breakthrough Questions Handout
- Cultural Proficiency Conceptual Framework Poster
- *Cultural Proficiency: A Manual for School Leaders* and *Culturally Proficient Inquiry: A Lens for Identifying and Examining Educational Gaps* books
- Projector
- Laptop
- Easel and sticky note paper
- 8 packs of 3" X 3" sticky notes

Resource C

Taniko's Poem

Defending My Destiny

I am more than a label!

You've grown accustomed to stereotyping me . . .

I make NO apologies for the LIFE

That was destiny for me!

I don't ask for your sympathy, merely a helping HAND

To assist me rather then underestimate me

In this battle for LIFE. Thus battle for answers

To so many questions that may validate or

Enhance the real me . . .

A new definition for my perception of living in HELL!

Consequently, the objectives were I'd undoubtedly FAIL . . .

And in this self-fulfilling prophecy I'd fight to excel!

Truth is, you know absolutely nothing about me!

You've obtained your perception based on what society

Tells you I should be!

My story, IRRELEVANT

My pain, FORTHRIGHT

My experiences have forced many people to take flight.

My sabotage, my fears, my anger, my tears

Have ALL gone unrecognized!

Instead you label me and force this WHITE man's

THEORY to "better understand me"!

Yet, time and time again your ears have been closed

Sincerely unable to listen.

Your power has afforded you to determine what's in

My "best interest."

However, you NEVER asked me what goals I had for my life.

You created programs that would determine the magnitude

Of MY light and whether or NOT my voice would be spoken!

Cries of frustration have inhibited my reluctance to believe in

YOU!

I'm bombarded with your "failed expectations," ANY non-compliance

Would force me again to experience REJECTION!

But you NEVER asked me how I wanted to live my LIFE!

And so, I thought I'd tell you IN MY OWN WORDS

And without any reservation, I AM DEFENDING MY SELF-MADE

DEFINITION . . .

I've determined my life is precious, it's a gift, and I intend to learn, love, and

Live it!

Not based on your opinion, but based on how I've determined and internally

Shaped my vision of REALITY.

I've been forced to rebuild the foundation of me AND so I

Walk with confidence and know I can DO & BE ANYTHING!

Resiliency is innate, it's already in me and although

I haven't lived the best of experiences they've each DEFINED

The essence of me.

So you may ask, why does her spoken word sound so angry and mad?!?

I'll shake my head because again, you'll try to analyze or personalize

My grief.

You'll attempt to "SAVE" me when this LIFE lesson is based on my

ABILITY to grow and be ENHANCED based on the discovery of

A reshaped me!

Adversity, oppression, lost identity, reshaping a life that

Unlocks my destiny is ONE of the reasons I've chosen to defend

The life journeys that define the future of me.

Babies out of wedlock, single-motherhood, victimization has ALL

Contributed to my aspirations, even in the midst of despair!

The cry to be different is my REVELATION,

Regardless of your desire to CARE!

I've used EDUCATION to empower MYSELF

THUS, the reason for my existing and REFUSING to FAIL.

Being motivated by a drug called KNOWLEDGE

Has created a lens that even SOCIETY can't dismantle.

Society has to accept, acknowledge, OR co-exist.

To adequately understand the dimensions that persist in me,

You gotta (got to) be less quick to judge & open to listen

Because a LABEL does NOT define me . . . I've created a self-Made

Definition.

I determine my DESTINY!

Source: Written by Taniko King. © 2007 All copyrights belong exclusively to Taniko King.

Resource D

How to Use the Cultural Proficiency Books

Book	Authors	Focus
Cultural Proficiency: A Manual for School Leaders, 3rd ed. (2009)	Randall B. Lindsey Kikanza Nuri-Robins Raymond D. Terrell	This book is an introduction to cultural proficiency. There is extended discussion of each of the tools and the historical framework for diversity work.
Culturally Proficient Instruction: A Guide for People Who Teach, 2nd ed. (2006)	Kikanza Nuri-Robins Randall B. Lindsey Delores B. Lindsey Raymond D. Terrell	This book focuses on the five essential elements and can be directed to anyone in an instructional role. This book can be used as a workbook for a study group.
The Culturally Proficient School: An Implementation Guide for School Leaders (2004)	Randall B. Lindsey Laraine M. Roberts Franklin CampbellJones	This book guides the reader to examine their school as a cultural organization and to design and implement approaches to dialogue and inquiry.
Culturally Proficient Coaching: Supporting Educators to Create Equitable Schools (2007)	Delores B. Lindsey Richard S. Martinez Randall B. Lindsey	This book aligns the essential elements with Costa and Garmston's Cognitive Coaching model. The book provides coaches, teachers, and administrators a personal guidebook with protocols and maps for conducting conversations that shift thinking in support of all students achieving at levels higher than ever before.
Culturally Proficient Inquiry: A Lens for Identifying and Examining Educational Gaps (2008)	Randall B. Lindsey Stephanie M. Graham R. Chris Westphal, Jr. Cynthia L. Jew	This book uses protocols for gathering and analyzing student achievement and access data as well as rubrics for gathering and analyzing data about educator practices. A CD accompanies the book for easy downloading and use of the data protocols.

Book	Authors	Focus
Culturally Proficient Leadership: The Personal Journey Begins Within (2009)	Raymond D. Terrell Randall B. Lindsey	This book guides the reader through the development of a cultural autobiography as a means to becoming an increasingly effective leader in our diverse society.
Culturally Proficient Learning Communities: Confronting Inequities Through Collaborative Curiosity (2009)	Delores B. Lindsey Linda D. Jungwirth Jarvis V.N.C. Pahl Randall B. Lindsey	This book provides readers a lens through which to examine the purpose, the intentions, and the progress of learning communities to which they belong, or wish to develop. School and district leaders are provided protocols, activities, and rubrics to engage in actions focused on the intersection of race, ethnicity, gender, social class, sexual orientation and identity, faith, and ableness with the disparities in student achievement.
The Cultural Proficiency Journey: Moving Beyond Ethical Barriers Toward Profound School Change (2010)	Franklin CampbellJones Brenda CampbellJones Randall B. Lindsey	This book explores cultural proficiency as an ethical construct. It makes transparent the connection between values, assumptions, and beliefs, and observable behavior making change possible and sustainable.
Culturally Proficient Education: An Asset-Based Response to Conditions of Poverty (2010)	Randall B. Lindsey Michelle S. Karns Keith Myatt	This book is designed for educators to learn how to identify and develop the strengths of students from low-income backgrounds.
Culturally Proficient Organizations: A Conversation With Colleagues About the Practice of Cultural Proficiency (working title; in press)	Kikanza Nuri-Robins Raymond D. Terrell Delores B. Lindsey Randall B. Lindsey	This book answers the question "How do you do it?" It is directed to managers and organizational leaders who want to introduce cultural proficiency systemically.

References

Associated Administrators of Los Angeles. (2008, September 1). *Update.* Los Angeles: Author.

Bandura, Albert. (1993). Perceived self-efficacy in cognitive development and functioning. *Educational Psychologist, 28*(2), 117–148.

Banks, James. (1999). *An introduction to multicultural education* (3rd ed.). Needham, MA: Allyn & Bacon.

Barton, Paul E., & Coley, Richard J. (2009). *Parsing the achievement gap II.* Princeton, NJ: Policy Information Center, Educational Testing Service.

Benard, Bonnie. (1991). *Fostering resiliency in kids: Protective factors in the family, school, and community.* Portland, OR: Western Regional Center for Drug-Free Schools and Communities.

Benard, Bonnie. (2004). *Resiliency: What we have learned.* Portland, OR: Western Regional Center for Drug-Free Schools and Communities.

Berliner, David. (2005). Our impoverished view of educational reform. *Teachers College Record, 108*(6), 949–995.

Berliner, David C. (2009). Poverty and potential: Out-of-school factors and school success. Retrieved May 17, 2009, from http://epicpolicy.org/publication/poverty-and-potential.

Biesta, Gert. (2007). Education and the democratic person: Toward a political conception of democratic education. *Teachers College Record, 109*(3).

Bloom, Janice L. (2007). (Mis)reading social class in the journey toward college: Youth development in urban America. *Teachers College Record, 109*(2), 343–368.

Books, Sue. (2004). *Poverty and schooling in the U.S.: Context and consequences.* New York: Lawrence Erlbaum and Associates, Taylor & Francis Group.

Bullock, Heather E., Williams, Wendy R., & Limbert, Wendy M. (2003). Predicting support for welfare policies: The impact of attributions and beliefs about inequality. *Journal of Poverty, 7,* 35–56.

Bureau of the Census. (2000). *School enrollment by race, Hispanic origin, and age and sex.* In statistical abstract of the United States (113th ed., Table 246, p. 155). Washington, DC: U.S. Government Printing Office.

CampbellJones, Brenda. (2002). Against the stream: White men who act in ways to eradicate racism and white privilege/entitlement in the United States of America. Unpublished doctoral dissertation. Claremont Graduate University.

Chenoweth, Karin. (2007). *It's being done: Academic success in unexpected schools*. Cambridge, MA: Harvard Education Press.

Children's Defense Fund. (2008). *The state of America's children 2008*. Washington, DC: Author.

Cross, Terry L., Bazron, Barbara J., Dennis, Karl W., & Isaacs, Mareasa R. (1989). *Toward a culturally competent system of care: Vol. 1*. Washington, DC: Georgetown University Child Development Program, Child and Adolescent Service System Program.

Darling-Hammond, Linda. (2004). Inequality and the right to learn: Access to qualified teachers in California's public schools. *Teachers College Record, 106*(10).

de Tocqueville, Alexis. (2001). *Democracy in America* (Richard C. Heffner, Ed.). East Rutherford, NJ: Penguin Group. (Original work published 1835)

Delpit, Lisa. (1995). *Other people's children*. New York: New York Press.

Dewey, John. (1916/1944). *Democracy and education: An introduction to the philosophy of education*. New York: Collier-Macmillan.

Dilts, Robert B. (1994). *Effective presentation skills*. Capitola, CA: Meta.

Ferguson, Ronald. (2007). *Toward excellence with equity: An emerging vision for closing the achievement gap*. Boston: Harvard Education Press.

Franklin, John Hope, & Moss, Alfred A., Jr. (1988). *From slavery to freedom: A history of negro Americans* (6th ed.). New York: McGraw-Hill.

Freire, Paulo. (1987). *Pedagogy of the oppressed*. New York: Continuum.

Freire, Paulo. (1995). *Pedagogy of hope. Reliving pedagogy of the oppressed*. New York: Continuum.

Freire, Paulo. (1998). *Pedagogy of hope: Reliving pedagogy of the oppressed*. New York: Continuum.

Fullan, Michael. (2003). *The moral imperative of school leadership*. Thousand Oaks, CA: Corwin.

Galster, George, & Killen, Sean. (1995). The geography of metropolitan opportunity: A reconnaissance and conceptual framework. *Housing Policy Debate, 6*(1), 7–43.

Garmezy, Norman. (1991). Resiliency and vulnerability to adverse developmental outcomes associated with poverty. *American Behavioral Scientist, 34*(4), 416–430.

Garmston, Robert J., & Wellman, Bruce M. (1999). *The adaptive school: A sourcebook for developing collaborative groups*. Norwood, MA: Christopher-Gordon Publishers.

Goddard, Rodger D., Hoy, Wayne K., & Hoy, Anita W. (2000). Collective teacher efficacy: Its meaning, measure, and effect on student achievement. *American Educational Research Journal, 37*(2), 479–507.

Gorski, Paul. (2008). The myth of the "culture of poverty." *Educational Leadership, 65*(7), 32.

Greenwood, Charles R. (1997). Classwide peer tutoring. *Behavior & Social Issues, 7*(1), 53–57.

Greenwood, Charles R., Delquadri, Joseph C., & Carta, Judith J. (1988). *Together we can: Classwide peer tutoring to improve basic academic skills*. Longmont, CO: Sopris West.

Gutstein, Eric. (2006). *Reading and writing the world with mathematics: Toward a pedagogy for social justice*. New York: Routledge.

Gutstein, Eric. (2007). And that's how it starts: Teaching mathematics and developing student agency. *Teachers College Record, 109*(2), 420–448.

Haberman, Martin. (1995). *Star teachers of children in poverty.* Irvine, CA: Kappa Delta Pi.

Haberman, Martin. (2005). *Star teachers.* Houston, TX: Haberman Educational Foundation.

Hanh, Thich Nhat. (1999). *Peace is every step.* New York: The Free Press.

Hederman, Rea S., Jr. (2008, August 27). Census bureau shows income gains in 2007, but poverty remains flat (Web Memo #2035). Washington, DC: The Heritage Foundation. Retrieved December 14, 2009, from http://www.heritage.org/Research/Welfare/wm2035.cfm. December 14, 2009.

Heifetz, Ronald A. (1994). *Leadership without easy answers.* Cambridge, MA: Belknap Press.

Hilliard, Asa. (1991). Do we have the will to educate all children? *Educational Leadership, 40*(1), 31–36.

Hollins, Etta. (2008). *Culture in school learning: Revealing the deep meaning.* New York: Routledge.

Howley, Craig B., Howley, Aimee A., Howley, Caitlin W., & Howley, Marge D. (2006, April). *Saving the children of the poor in rural schools.* Paper presented at the American Educational Research Association.

Hoy, Wayne K., Tarter, C. John, & Hoy, Anita Woolfolk. (2006). Academic optimism of schools: A force for student achievement. *American Educational Research Journal, 43,* 425–446.

Jerald, Craig D. (2007). Believing and achieving [Electronic version]. *The Center for Comprehensive School Reform and Improvement's Issue Brief,* 1–6. Retrieved October 2, 2007, from http://www.centerforcsri.org.

Jones, Ian. (2009, July 9). *Culturally proficient student leadership at Milton High School, Ontario, Canada.* Paper presented at the Cultural Proficiency Institute, 4th Annual.

Katznelson, Ira. (2005). *When affirmative action was white: An untold history of racial inequality in twentieth-century America.* New York: Norton, W. W. & Company.

Kendall, Joseph S., & Marzano, Robert J. (2004). *Content knowledge: A compendium of standards and benchmarks for K–12 education.* Retrieved August 30, 2009, from Mid-continent Research for Education and Learning: http://www.mcrel.org/standards-benchmarks/.

Keyssar, Alexander. (2002). *The contested history of democracy in the United States.* New York: Basic Books.

Kovel, Joel. (1984). *White racism: A psychohistory.* New York: Columbia, University Press.

Ladson-Billings, Gloria. (1994). *The dreamkeepers: Successful teachers of African American children.* San Francisco: Jossey-Bass.

Lawson, Michael A. (2003). School-family relations in context: Parent and teacher perceptions of parent involvement. *Urban Education, 38*(1), 77–133.

Lemann, Nicholas. (1999). *The big test: The secret history of American meritocracy.* New York: Farrar, Straus, and Giroux.

Lewis, Oscar. (1959). *Five families.* New York: Basic Books.

Lewis, Oscar. (1961). *The children of Sanchez: Autobiography of a Mexican family.* New York: Random House.

Lindsey, Randall B., Graham, Stephanie M., Westphal, R. Chris, Jr., & Jew, Cynthia L. (2008). *Culturally proficient inquiry: A lens for identifying and examining educational groups.* Thousand Oaks, CA: Corwin.

Lindsey, Randall B., Nuri-Robins, Kikanza, Terrell, Raymond D. (2009). *Culturally Proficient Inquiry: A Manual for School Leaders (3rd).* Thousand Oaks, CA: Corwin.

Love, Nancy. (2009). *Using data to improve learning for all: A collaborative inquiry approach.* Thousand Oaks, CA: Corwin.

Masten, Ann S. (2001). Ordinary magic: Resilience processes and development. *American Psychologist, 56,* 227–238.

Melville, Herman. (2009). *The globe and mail.* Toronto, Ontario: CTVglobemedia Publishing.

Moser, Geraldine O. N. (2006). *Asset-based approaches to poverty reduction in a globalized context: An introduction to asset accumulation policy and summary of workshop findings.* Washington, DC: The Brookings Institution.

National Policy Board for Educational Administration. (2008). *Educational leadership policy standards: ISLLC 2008.* Washington, DC: Council of Chief State School Officers.

No Child Left Behind Act of 2001. Public Law 108–110, 20 U.S.C. § 6301 et seq. (2002). Retrieved from http://www.ed.gov/nclb/landing.jhtml.

Noddings, Nell. (2003). *Caring: A feminine approach to ethics and moral education.* Berkeley, CA: University of California Press.

Nuri-Robins, Kikanza, Lindsey, Randall B., Lindsey, Delores B., and Terrell, Raymond D. (2006).*Culturally proficient instruction: A guide for people who teach* (2nd ed.). Thousand Oaks, CA: Corwin.

Ontario Ministry of Education. (2009). *Realizing the promise of diversity: Ontario's equity and inclusive education strategy.* Ottawa: Ministry of Education.

Passel, Jeffrey S., & Cohn, D'Vera. (2008, October). *Trends in unauthorized immigration: Undocumented inflow now trails legal inflow.* Washington, DC: Pew Hispanic Center.

Paxis Institute. (2001). *Paxis Institute, productivity, peace, health, happiness.* Retrieved from http://www.paxis.org/.

Payne, R. K. (2005). *A framework for understanding poverty* (4th rev. ed.). Highlands, TX: aha! Process.

Payne, Ruby K. (2009, May 17). Using the lens of economic class to help teachers understand and teach students from poverty: A response. *Teachers College Record.*

Perie, Marianne, Moran, Rebecca, & Lutkus, Anthony D. (2005). *NAEP 2004 trends in academic progress: Three decades of student performance in reading and mathematics.* Washington, DC: U.S. Government Printing Office.

Pogrow, Stanley. (2009, February). Accelerating the learning of 4th and 5th graders born into poverty. *Phi Delta Kappan, 90*(6), 408–412.

Prins, Esther, & Schaft, Kai A. (2009). Individual and structural attributions for poverty and persistence in family literacy programs: The resurgence of the culture of poverty. *Teachers College Record, 111*(9).

Rank, Mark R. (2004). *One nation underprivileged: Why American poverty affects us all.* New York: Oxford University Press.

Ross, John A., & Gray, Peter. (2006). Transformational leadership and teacher commitment to organizational values: The mediating effects of collective teacher efficacy. *School Effectiveness and School Improvement, 17*(2), 179–199.

Rothstein, Richard. (2008). Whose problem is poverty? *Educational Leadership, 65*(7), 8–13.

Rutter, Michael. (1978). Family, area, and school influences in the genesis of conduct disorders. In Lionel Abraham Hersov, M. Berger, & David Shaffe (Eds.), *Aggression and anti-social behavior in childhood and adolescence* (pp. 95–114). Oxford: Pergamon.

Rutter, Michael. (1987). Psychosocial resilience and protective mechanism. *American Journal of Orthopsychiatry, 57,* 316–331.

Sanders, Nancy M., & Kearney, Karen M. (2008). *Performance expectations and indicators for education leaders.* Washington, DC: Council of Chief State School Officers.

Scales, Peter C., Benson, Peter L., Roehlkepartain, Eugene C., Sesma, Arturo, Jr., & van Dulmen, Manfred. (2006, October). The role of developmental assets in predicting academic achievement: A longitudinal study. *Journal of Adolescence, 29*(5), 691–708.

Senge, Peter, Cambron McCabe, Nelda H., Lucas, Timothy, Kleiner, Art, Dutton, Janis, & Smith, Bryan. (2000). *Schools that learn: A fifth discipline fieldbook for educators, parents, and everyone who cares about education.* New York: Doubleday.

Sesma, Arturo, Jr., & Roehlkepartain, Eugene C. (2003, November). Unique strengths, shared strengths: Developmental assets among youth of color. *Insights and Evidence, 1*(1), 1.

Shapiro, Joan Poliner, & Stefkovich, Jacqueline A. (2005). *Ethical leadership and decision making in education: Applying theoretical perspectives to complex dilemmas* (2nd ed.). Mahway, NJ: Lawrence Erlbaum Associates.

Skrla, Linda, McKenzie, Kathryn Bell, & Scheurich, James Joseph. (2009). *Using equity audits to create equitable and excellent schools.* Thousand Oaks, CA: Corwin.

Smith-Lever Cooperative Extension Act. (1914). Retrieved from http://www.ca.uky.edu/agripedia/glossary/smithlev.htm.

Spring, Joel (2006). *American education* (12th ed.). Boston: McGraw-Hill.

Takaki, Ronald. (1991, May–June). The content of the curriculum: Two views: The value of multiculturalism. *Liberal Education, 77,* 9–10.

Terrell, Raymond D., & Lindsey, Randall B. (2009). *Culturally proficient leadership: The journey begins within.* Thousand Oaks, CA: Corwin.

Turner, Sarah, & Bound, John. (2002, July). *Closing the gap or widening the divide: The effects of the G.I. Bill and World War II on the educational outcomes of black Americans.* Cambridge, MA: National Bureau of Economic Research.

U.S. Department of Health & Human Services. (2009, January). Annual Salary Poverty Guidelines, 74 Fed. Reg. 4199–4201.

Valencia, Richard R. (2009, June 25). A response to Ruby Payne's claim that the deficit thinking model has no scholarly utility. *Teachers College Record.*

Weigt, Jill. (2006). Compromises to carework: The social organization of mother's experiences in the low wage labor market after welfare reform. *Social Problems, 53*(3), 332–351.

Werner, Emmy E., & Smith, Ruth S. (1982). *Vulnerable but invincible: A longitudinal study of resilient children and youth.* New York: Adams, Bannister, and Cox.

Werner, Emmy E., & Smith, Ruth S. (1992). *Overcoming the odds: High-risk children from birth to adulthood.* New York: Cornell University Press.

Werner, Emmy E.., & Smith, Ruth S. (2001). *Journeys from childhood to midlife: Risk, resilience, and recovery.* Ithaca, NY: Cornell University Press.

Wheatley, Margaret. (2002). *Turning to one another: Simple conversations to restore hope to the future.* San Francisco: Berrett-Koehler.

Wiggington, Eliot. (1972). *Sometimes a shining moment: The foxfire experience. Twenty years teaching in a high school classroom.* New York: Anchor Books, Anchor Press/Doubleday.

Wilkins, Amy. (2006). *Yes we can: Telling truths and dispelling myths about race and education in America.* Washington, DC: The Education Trust.

Suggested Additional Readings

Anderson, Lorin W., & Krathwohl, David R. (Eds.). (2001). *A taxonomy for learning, teaching, and assessing: A revision of Bloom's taxonomy of educational objectives.* New York: Longman.

Bar, Robert D., & Parrett, William. (2007). *Saving our students, saving our schools.* Thousand Oaks, CA Corwin.

Bloom, Benjamin S. (1956). *Taxonomy of educational objectives, handbook I: The cognitive domain.* New York: David McKay.

Bryk, Anthony S., & Schneider, Barbara. (2003). Trust in schools: A core resource for school reform. *Educational Leadership, 60*(6), 40–45.

Cengage, Gale. (1995). *1940s education: Teacher shortages and strikes* [Electronic version]. Retrieved May 2009 from www.enotes.com/1940-education-american-decades/teacher-shortages-strikes.

Collins, Denis E. (1977). *Paulo Freire: His life, works, and thought.* New York: Paulist Press.

Cruz, Emily. (2003). Bloom's revised taxonomy. *Encyclopedia of Educational Technology.*

Dilts, Robert B. (1990). *Changing belief systems with NLP.* Capitola, CA: Meta.

EdTrust. (2004). Achievement rises and gaps narrow, but too slowly. Retrieved October 2004, from http://www2.edtrust.org.

Elmore, Richard F. (2000). *Building a new structure for school leadership.* The Albert Shanker Institute.

Freire, Paulo. (2001). *Pedagogy of freedom: Ethics, democracy, and civic courage.* New York: Rowman and Littlefield.

Gilligan, Carol. (1983). *In a different voice.* Cambridge, MA: Harvard University Press.

Glatthorn, Allan A., & Jailall, Jerry. (2008). *The principal as curriculum leader: Shaping what is taught and tested.* Thousand Oaks, CA: Corwin.

Goddard, Rodger D., Hoy, Wayne K., & Hoy, Anita W. (2004, April). Collective efficacy beliefs: Theoretical developments, empirical evidence, and future directions. *Educational Researcher, 33*(3), 3–13.

Good, Thomas C., & Weinstein, Rhonda S. (1986). Teacher expectations: A framework for exploring classrooms. *Improving Teaching, ASCD Yearbook,* 63–85.

Gudrais, Elizabeth. (2008, July–August). Unequal America: Causes and consequences of the wide—and growing—gap between rich and poor. *Harvard Magazine, 110*(6), 22–29.

Haberman, Martin. (1996). Selecting and preparing culturally competent teachers for urban schools. *Handbook of Research on Teacher Education,* 747–760.

Hopkins, Eric. (2000). *Industrialization and society.* New York: Routledge.

Irvine, Jacqueline Jordan. (1991). *Black students and school failure: Policies, practices, and prescriptions.* New York: Greenwood Publishing Group.

Isaacs, Julia B., Sawhill, Isabel V., & Haskins, Ron. (2008). *Getting ahead or losing ground: Economic mobility in America.* Washington, DC: The Brookings Institution.

Karns, Michelle, & Blake, Toni. (1998). *Ethnic barriers and biases: How to become an agent for change.* Sebastopol, CA: National Training Associates.

Kearney, Karen. (2003). *Moving leadership standards into everyday work: Descriptions of practice:* Oakland, CA: Wested.

Kliebard, Herbert M. (2004). *The struggle for the American curriculum, 1893–1958* (3rd ed.). New York: Routledge.

Krathwohl, David R., Bloom, Benjamin S., & Masia, Bertram B. (1973). *Taxonomy of educational objectives, the classification of educational goals, handbook II: Affective domain.* New York: David McKay.

Lindsey, Randall. B., Nuri-Robins, Kikanza, & Terrell, Raymond D. (2003). *Cultural proficiency: A manual for school leaders* (2nd ed.). Thousand Oaks, CA: Corwin.

Marzano, Robert, Pickering, Debra, & Pollack, Jane. (2001). *Classroom instruction that works.* Alexandria, VA: Association for Supervision and Curriculum Development.

Maslow, Abraham H. (1998). *Toward a psychology of being* (3rd ed.). New York: Wiley.

Masterson, Margaret. (1970). The nature of a paradigm. In Imre Lakatos and Alan Musgrave (Eds.), *Criticism and the growth of knowledge* (pp. 59–89). Cambridge: Cambridge University Press.

McKenzie, Katherine B., & Scheurich, James J. (2004). Equity traps: A useful construct for preparing principals to lead schools that are successful with racially diverse students. *Educational Administration Quarterly, 40*(5), 601–632.

Miller, Kathleen K., Crandall, Mindy S., & Weber, Bruce A. (2002). *Persistent poverty and place: How do persistent poverty and poverty demographics vary?* Paper presented at the Economic Research Service of the U.S. Department of Agriculture.

National Education Association. (1959, April). Financial incentives for teachers. *Research Bulletin, 37.*

Pesek, Dolores D., & Kirshner, Davis. (2000). Interference of instrumental instruction in subsequent relational learning. *Journal for Research in Mathematics Education, 31*(5), 524–540.

Peters, David J. (2009). Typology of American poverty. *International Regional Science Review, 32*(19), 19–39.

Pogrow, Stanley. (2004, October 3). The missing element in reducing the learning gap: Eliminating the "blank stare." *Teachers College Record.*

Reeves, Douglas B. (2006). *The learning leader: How to focus school improvement for better results.* Alexandria, VA: Association for Supervision and Curriculum Development.

Sanders, Nancy, & Simpson, Joe. (2005). *State policy framework to develop highly qualified educational administrators.* Washington, DC: Council of Chief State School Officers.

Schein, Edgar H. (2004). *Organizational culture and leadership.* San Francisco: Jossey-Bass.

Seligman, Martin (with Reivich, Karen, Jaycox, Lisa H., & Gillham, Jane). (1995). *Optimistic child: A revolutionary program that safeguards children against depression and builds lifelong resiliency.* New York: Houghton-Mifflin.

Shakeshaft, Charol, Sarason, Seymour B., & Shaker, Paul. (2004, September). Big change question: What is needed to resolve the social and critical issues affecting large scale reform? Macro change demands micro involvement. *Journal of Educational Change, 5*(3), 292–295.

Sinclair, Robert L., & Ghory, Ward J. (1987). *Reaching marginal students: Primary concern for school renewal.* Berkeley, CA: McCutchan Publishing.

Temin, Peter. (2002, April). *Teacher quality and the future of America.* Paper presented at the NBER Working Paper.

Urban Dictionary "street cred." (2009). Retrieved September 13, 2009, from http://www.urbandictionary.com/define.php?term=street%20cred.

Ward, Randolph E., & Burke, Mary Ann. (2004). *Improving achievement in low-performing schools.* Thousand Oaks, CA: Corwin.

Werner, Emmy E. (1996, Winter). How children become resilient. *Resiliency in Action: A Journal of Application and Research, 1*(1), 18–28.

Wheatley, Margaret. (1992). *Leadership and the new science.* San Francisco: Berrett-Koehler.

Index

CORWIN

A SAGE Company

The Corwin logo—a raven striding across an open book—represents the union of courage and learning. Corwin is committed to improving education for all learners by publishing books and other professional development resources for those serving the field of PreK–12 education. By providing practical, hands-on materials, Corwin continues to carry out the promise of its motto: **"Helping Educators Do Their Work Better."**

AMERICAN ASSOCIATION OF SCHOOL ADMINISTRATORS

The American Association of School Administrators, founded in 1865, is the professional organization for more than 13,000 educational leaders across the United States. AASA's mission is to support and develop effective school system leaders who are dedicated to the highest quality public education for all children. For more information, visit www.aasa.org.